Almost To My Grave Reviews

The most courageous piece of w
I have ever read. If Huck Finn
molested as children this might b

—Robert Rogers Business Owner
and a friend to a family whose children
are survivors of child sexual molestation

It is said that to love God you must hate evil. It is difficult for the mind to contemplate anything more evil than the taking of a child's innocence, self-worth and hope. It is even more difficult, to be the victim of this most loathsome of the loathsome behavior, recover from it and return to normalcy to lead a productive life. And, it is most extraordinary that having done so, to dedicate your life to helping the most damaged amongst us find their way back. That is what this book is about.

If your experience in the life has been like mine, this book is an expose of a world that exists beyond the parameters and understanding that most of us ever imagined. It is not a "tell-all book" although it does in fact tell all. It is not a condemnation of many of the institutions that we know and many of us love. To understand that I quote the great Viktor Frankel, who after surviving the horrors of a Nazi concentration camp wrote, "From all of this we may learn that there are two races of men in this world, but only these two—the "race" of the decent man and the "race" of the indecent man. Both are found everywhere; they penetrate into all groups of society. No group consists entirely of decent or indecent people." If your experience however, has been that of a "victim" this book is a lifeline and a promise of restoration to your damaged soul. But regardless of which category you fit into two truths will emerge. Pedophilia is an epidemic that must be addressed and Ray Bilodeau hates evil and loves God!

—John Williamson Attorney at Law

A book of survival and perseverance, complex family relationships and the dark underbelly of one of America's darkest secrets of organized child abuse. Almost To My Grave by Raymond Bilodeau is a riveting look at his childhood memories of his child abuse. It chronicles and highlights Raymond's determination and efforts to make his abuser stand accountable for the abuse he inflicted on Ray and of the hundreds of other children this individual harmed. Culminating with an L.A.P.D. sting operation and Mr. Bilodeau wearing a wire during a meeting with his abuser. This book is raw with emotion and you can't help but keep turning the page. A candid look at the experience of one 12 year old who experienced things no child should ever have to. 5 stars

—Billy Petitt, Survivor of child sexual abuse

Raymond takes his readers on a painstaking journey through a lifetime that has been horrendously affected by unspeakable and often violent child abuse. From a young boy desperately trying to survive from one day to the next, to a grown man trying to cope with the memories of the abuse that he almost succumbed to.

It is an eye opening accounting of how he survived a vicious monster, the kind that most of us could never imagine. I am so grateful to Raymond for having the courage and determination to write this book. Everyone should read it, especially parents of young children. His writings teach us how important it is to protect our children, and that the monsters are closer than you think. Once I started reading, I couldn't put it down.

As a husband who's wife was a victim of child abuse, I know the toll it takes even into adulthood, and the roll it plays in future relationships. It casts a shadow of darkness on humanity that makes it difficult to trust.

We should be grateful to Raymond for telling his story and helping to bring this subject out of the shadows and into the forefront. We need more laws to protect the victims of child abuse. Our society has protected the predators way too long.

This book is about one man's fight, to not only survive, but to also move forward. Chilling!!!

**—Husband of wife
who was sexually abused as a child**

Almost To My Grave is an intimate, eye opening, first hand account of the ongoing epidemic of sexual abuse that is pervasive amongst society today. Written from the perspective of a survivor dealing with the intense suffering and trauma he experienced. The author takes us into a world that many of us have chosen not to see—either by innocent foolishness or intentional ignorance—a terrifying reality for 30 million sexual abuse victims in the United States alone.

From first hand encounters with a prolific pedophile, to the agony experienced while dealing with these experiences as an adult, to the author's obsessive path to redemption... I definitely recommend Almost To My Grave as it will open the eyes of the deniers to a dark world that has destroyed so many youth's lives.

**—Richard Nevitt,
friend of a survivor of child sexual abuse**

As uncomfortable as this story is to read it is even harder to live through... then tell it. Not everyone can do that and that is exactly what the abusers hope for... silence, fear, shame.

I applaud Ray for being brave enough to put a face to this horrible, hidden epidemic. In today's society it is a difficult discussion let alone a difficult read about abuse on many levels. The abused need to feel that their voices matter.

—Desiree Vidal, Business Owner

An easy reading page turning book. A raw description of a child's predator actions. A constant reminder of the dangers surrounding us in our daily lives.

How we are always concerned on how to protect our children from the dangers outside, when at times the monster is already inside. How come our society is not able to identify and stop this type of crime from happening? How could John Dark be able to live a full circle of life of crime and abuse? It took the courage of one brave victim to bring this monster down to justice.

—Survivor of child sexual abuse

Almost To My Grave

Almost To My Grave

A Memoir

Raymond Bilodeau

ISBN Paperback: 978-0-578-61072-6
ISBN eBook: 978-0-578-61073-3

Printed in the United States of America

Editor: Celia Pool
Cover and Interior Design: Ghislain Viau

Contents

Introduction

My life was ending, with no time, I had to murder. No one went the distance, no one thought of the consequences, only a few were brave enough to try, but the entire system failed, and more would lose their souls. A life of trying to forget and run, I had nowhere left to go. I had nothing left to live for. I must try until the day I die. If I could just somehow think straight, stop crying, stop remembering, stop these nightmares. I needed to eat, I needed to sleep, I needed help. Almost everywhere I turned I was shunned, I was cast aside, I was even disbelieved. I almost ran out of faith. Once I reconnected I was shown a path to follow. With more than forty years for this predator to roam, we prevailed, where all others failed.

In the heat of passion, I could of. In the calm cool silence and only a few feet away, I realized that I did not possess the ability for cold blooded murder. Was I a coward? I have shown courage most of my life. The voice of attorney John Williamson was ringing in my mind, "Is there another way?" I went back to my vehicle holding my loaded 44 Magnum handgun in my hands. After I tracked him down and we held our stare out that night, I planned this. I picked the gun, I picked the ammo, I picked the location. This would be up close and personal, this would be no near miss, this would be a mess. Tonight I could not, perhaps later.

I had not realized that not only my memories, but my burning rage had also been repressed. I somehow figured out a way to channel my extreme anger, into the pursuit of stopping this vicious child sexual predator. I would of never dreamed of how many obstacles, and how long this would take. It is quoted "Before you embark on a journey of revenge, dig two graves". Revenge was not in my heart, stopping this evil person from causing any more carnage to the souls of our children, was always my drive. I did not yet need my grave, but this journey cost me dearly. With all of the pain, with all of the frustration, with all of the costs, would I do this again? Unequivocally Yes! I saved children, I will never know who they were, or how many there were, but I saved children, and this feels good.

When my job was finished, I so wanted to just forget it all again, and go back as before when I had no knowledge of my past. I slowly crawled back inside of my body, with more and more of me shutting out this world. By chance I met and married my lovely wife Joanna, who saved and changed my life. Joanna helped me cure myself of cancer without the surgery and other treatments that the Doctors were pushing me to do. During the first five years of our marriage, Joanna had no knowledge of this story.

I did not want to feel, think, or talk about these past traumas, so why write this book? Weslee my son, was asking me if he could record my story. I did not want to do this, but Weslee kept asking, and he had saved a copy of that speech given in 2003 by the Los Angeles District Attorney's office. After so many years of psychotherapy, and not talking much about my childhood rape and sexual molestation, I desperately did not want to share my shame and my pain with my son. However, I was feeling internal anxiety to release this pressure. July 31, 2018 I wrote my first paragraph, and shared this with a little world of people, including my son Weslee. I received back overwhelming encouragement to finish this story. Some of these people were victims themselves of rape or childhood sexual molestation. Some of these people were parents of children who had been sexually molested. Some other people said that they were simply not aware of the pervasiveness of these horrific crimes being perpetrated on our children. One person said to me that I was a voice for them. As I was remembering and writing, I was changing. After more than 50 years, I no longer needed to hug a pillow. My nightmares were leaving me, and I was waking up less and less drenched.

Besides my bad memories, I was remembering good memories. I was trying to come to grips as to how I had gotten myself into that terrible situation in the first place. I followed myself from a little boy with so much hope and interest in life, to an older broken boy. I saw an older boy who turned into a man who had become withdrawn and overly serious. I saw a man who became a workaholic and did not spend enough time with his family. Time went by so fast and his children were grown. I could feel his pain, and sorrow, and his desire to end his own life.

I will walk us through a journey of hunting down a monster, who Susan Freeman of the Los Angeles District Attorney's office claimed was the most prolific child molester aware of in America. I will talk about how my life changed after putting John Dark to rest.

Besides writing I have spent much of this past year researching the devastating effects on our minds and bodies, from these terrible experiences endured in our society. The costs to America alone is staggering, from the carnage done by these horrible child molesters.

I write this book for my late mom and dad who were themselves victims of childhood sexual molestation. I write this book for my older sister Debbie. Debbie would hold my hand in our youth like a young mom, but being only one year and two days older than me. Being separated by a door we could not see each other, but we could hear the pain being inflicted on us by our father, while kneeling in our corners. I write this book for my younger sister Alberta. Alberta endured hardships in her life, from being part of our traumatized family. I write this book for my younger brother Albert, who was himself a victim of childhood sexual molestation, from the same man as me. The same brother who was sucked into being a child prostitute, and was sold to Hollywood, the Catholic church, and rich business people. I have written this book for the more than forty million victims and survivors like myself in America. I have written this book to the parents, and families who had children who were victims of this horrific crime.

This disease we call child sexual molestation, is still happening unabated in America. We need a much more effective way of communicating this information within our society, then we seem to be doing now. Our history in this area seems to keep repeating itself, and we keep paying for this.

I am grateful to many people for the constant encouragement to keep writing this story. Firstly, if not for my wonderful wife Joanna, I most likely would of been long gone. Without my son Weslee saving that speech, and his constant gentle pressure, there would be no book. During my pursuit of John Dark, one family who also had a child who was a victim of this animal, became my friends, and part of my support team. This family would like to remain anonymous. John Williamson my friend, has been a great supporter of mine. Thank You Tina, you encourage me, and you were part of the second sting operation. Thank you Richard, Matt, Chris, Chris jr. Billy, John, Bob. Thank You State Senator Cathy Wright and her staff. Thank you Los Angeles assistant district attorney Susan Freeman. Thank you Assistant Head Deputy Irene Wakabayashi. Thank You very much Detective Kevin Becker, and all of the Los Angeles Police Department.

Assistant Head Deputy Irene Wakabayashi
Courageous Citizen Awards Ceremony
April 25, 2003

It was 1996, and doctors told Ray he only had two years to live. He didn't really question the prognosis. After all, he was a workaholic and had been suffering from several blood, nervous system, and breathing afflictions. He also suffered memory loss, having repressed blocks of childhood memories. But that would all soon change.

Early the next year, Ray's mom told him that a childhood friend had called her looking for him. It had been over 25 years since Ray had spoken to his friend, but hearing from his friend triggered something that would change his life forever. Suddenly, the repressed memories of Ray's adolescence began to come back to him.

Our honoree remembered that as a 12-year-old in 1967, he was sexually molested by the scoutmaster of his Boy Scouts troop. And he remembered that it was not a one-time occurrence. In fact, Ray remembered that his abuser had molested him on a regular basis for over three years.

Ray also remembered that he was not this man's only victim. This abuser had a well-established M.O. He infiltrated several organizations to meet young boys – the Boy Scouts, little league, religious institutions, and youth clubs. He then befriended the boys' families. When he was accepted by the young boys and their families, he molested and raped them. And no one said a thing.

Within a few days of his horrific memory recall, our honoree had a nervous breakdown. He began suffering from uncontrollable shakes. He lost 30 pounds within a few weeks. He tried everything he could to get one or two hours of sleep a night.

But one thing that could not be broken down was Ray's strength and courage. He began therapy. And channeling the rage he felt toward his abuser, he resolved not to let his abuser hurt anyone else anymore. Somehow, he generated the inner strength and courage to pursue his abuser.

Our honoree hired a private investigator to help him in his quest for justice. The investigator helped him locate the sexual predator, while Ray searched for more proof of the man's abusive nature.

For months, Ray searched the internet for other victims. He trailed his abuser six days a week. But every time he found some corroborating information, the private investigator told him he needed more.

So Ray decided to follow the trail of older victims he remembered from his childhood. Contacting victims and their families led to more victims. The path of destruction left by this sexual predator was enormous. But still, the private investigator said he needed more. Our honoree began to get frustrated.

In May of 1997, Ray wrote to the District Attorney's Office for help. We connected him with LAPD's Detective Kevin Becker, [who is here today.]

Ray soon learned from Detective Becker that his private investigator was actually an LAPD officer who'd defrauded him. The con artist, whom our office ultimately prosecuted for fraud, had bilked Ray out of tens of thousands of dollars.

But while Ray's private investigator had turned out to be a fraud, his determination to put his abuser behind bars never wavered. With Detective Becker now at his side, Ray continued his search for more proof. Because of Ray's unbelievable courage, that proof came directly from his abuser.

Working with Detective Becker, Ray left a note on the sexual predator's truck one day asking him for a chance to talk. The plan worked, but not completely. Though the man called Ray, he wouldn't say anything to implicate himself over the phone.

So Ray took a difficult next step. He wore a wire and on two separate occasions met face to face with the man who had tormented him 30 years before. Ray pretended to befriend the man. Unaware that he was under video and audio surveillance, the man talked about the abuse he inflicted on Ray and on multiple other victims. Somehow, someway, our honoree got the man to admit to his horrendous career of child molestation.

The man's admission on video and audio tape cleared the way for a successful prosecution. Six other victims ultimately gave formal statements to the police. Deputy District Attorney Suzanne Freeman charged the man with 54 counts of sexual abuse. He pleaded guilty to several of them and was sentenced to 15 years in state prison. Because of his age and physical illness, he will surely never walk our streets again.

Every corner Ray turned in his quest for justice was fraught with mental, emotional, and physical anguish. In all, Ray's search turned up at least 78 people victimized by this man over his 30-plus year molestation career. Somehow, our honoree found the inner strength to continue. As he said recently, "Every time I found a new family destroyed by this man, it made me more determined."

That determination has put away a dangerous sexual predator for life – a remarkable feat on its own. But what Ray did goes far beyond that. He's talking about his experience. He's willing to be honored in a public ceremony. He's serving as an inspiration to others who have suffered similar trauma.

Page 7 of 9

Moreover, largely because of our honoree, laws are being improved so that past episodes of sexual abuse can be prosecuted. In the past couple of years, the clergy abuse scandal has changed the way people look at old sexual abuse cases. But in many ways, our honoree set the precedent for pursuing such cases on his own. Doing so, he's helped pave the way to justice and healing for other victims.

If you talk to Ray, he'll tell you how grateful he is for the encouragement and resources given by Detective Becker. He'll thank the other victims who came forward. And we join him in both those sentiments.

But we also join victims everywhere in thanking Ray. He's faced his greatest fears and spent considerable financial resources, time, blood, sweat, and tears to take a monstrous man off the streets. His life, he says, is dramatically better for it. We know that so many other lives will be dramatically better for it, as well.

So on behalf of the District Attorney's Office, the people of Los Angeles County, and the People of the State of California, it's my pleasure to present Ray Bilodeau with the Courageous Citizen Award.

Page 9 of 9

CHAPTER 1

Childhood

1997

Here I was in the dark of night, standing at the curb, under an old-style streetlight, in front of his home in Alhambra, California. Here lived the man who, more than three decades ago, stole my laughter, my innocence, my zest for life, and almost my soul. The lights were on and the curtains were drawn open. After almost 30 years of not seeing or thinking of him, John Dark appeared. I had no feeling of excitement, no anger, no fear, no emotion at all, just total indifference. He looked outside, and like in an eerie movie, he drew himself closer and closer to his open window, all the while, his gaze was intently focused on me. As if in a dream, I was staring eyeball to eyeball with the face of pure evil. He would not remove his eyes from me, nor I from him. So many victims: Johnny, Eric, Mark, Peter, Hank, George, Harry, Jim, Jay, another Eric, Jacob, Jordan, Jordan's brother, Jordan's other brother, my brother, myself, etcetera, etcetera, etcetera. In a flash it came, I knew right then and there what I was going to do. I am going to kill this man. Would I be able to get to him before he retrieved a weapon and I was stopped?

#

On one unfortunate occasion, I was sitting at someone's home on a folding chair, oblivious to the party that was going on around me. John Dark had brought me there for some unknown reason. As John Dark was mingling with other people at this party, he made eye contact with me. He made a gesture for me to follow him into another room. The party, the people talking, were all there for me to hear as he pulled my pants down, and I was sodomized. I think that this may have been the 50th or 80th time. I do not remember, but I was 13 at the time. I pulled my pants back up, and I went straight back to my folding chair. It seemed that all of the people there were looking at me, but by this time, I could barely feel anything anymore. Even as his semen was leaking from me, I could barely feel. By the next morning, the memory of this, like all of the other times, was buried.

#

June 6, 1954, at the Lakes Region General Hospital in Laconia, New Hampshire, I reluctantly arrived into this world. I was in no hurry to leave the safety of my original home, so forceps were used to extract me. For many, many years, I had two scars from that procedure, but they have since disappeared. We were good children, maybe just a little bit mischievous, but good children. We never did anything serious enough to earn what the future had in store for us, like millions of other children who have lived the same fate as my brother and I did.

My mother's name was Roberta Bilodeau; Granger was her maiden name. My father's name was Leon Bilodeau. I have a sister, Debbie Bilodeau, born one year and two days before me. I had a brother, Albert Bilodeau, born almost one and one-half years after me. I had a sister, Alberta Bilodeau, born about six years after me. My father's father, Joseph Bilodeau, had a business called Gilford Plumbing and Heating. My grandfather had a nice home with a bit of property in Gilford, New Hampshire, which was not far from where I was born. After my parents gave birth to my older sister, my grandfather had another home built on his property. After my mother became pregnant with me, my grandfather added another bedroom to that house. My grandfather then approached my mom and dad and offered my father a job working with him, and a home for us all to live in.

After I arrived in this world, there was a nice new home for my parents to take me to. For the first 8 years of my life, we enjoyed a very comfortable lifestyle. My older sister, and later my brother, loved to play outdoors. I do not have many fond memories of inside the house, except for my mom's cooking. I loved her pancakes, pizza, and donuts. However, I did not like her baked beans at all. My older sister hated the smell of my mom's pizza; when my mom would bake a pizza, she would cry. The funny thing is that she liked to eat this pizza. I guess that we are all strange, in one way or another. We loved to play in the snow in the winter, we loved the spring, we loved the fall, we loved the summer. My brother and I especially loved watching and catching fireflies. My brother and I would also go for long walks together.

VW built a dealership near us, and during the construction, they accumulated a very large pile of dirt. My brother and I would play and roll down this giant dirt pile. When VW opened up their showroom, my brother and I would sometimes hang out there, and we were never asked to leave by the VW staff. The employees many times would give us a little VW, which was like a matchbox car, which was so cool. Except for our father, we never had one single person act mean towards us.

My brother and I thought that it would be fun to chase our neighbor's chickens, but we soon learned that this was a mistake. Some of them would chase back, and peck, and we ended up being chased. While I think back now, I believe that one or two of them were roosters. My brother and I would steal carrots from our neighbor's garden, very thick and very sweet carrots. The lady who owned the garden, Miss Sargent, did not say anything to us. One day on a carrot run, Miss Sargent came out and asked me if I wanted to ride on her goat, and this seemed exciting. She held the goat and helped me on. When she let the goat loose the goat started to run. The goat wanted me off, so I was on my ass fast. Miss Sargent asked me if I was okay, and did I want to ride her goat again. I did not ride her goat again, and my brother and I did not raid her garden ever again.

Until Albert grew older, my older sister Debbie and I were like two peas in a pod. My brother Albert and I started to do more together, which I now feel caused stress for my sister. In that home though, the three of us played well together. The weekends were especially stressful for us three kids. My dad drank alcohol and stayed up late on the weekends, and he wanted to sleep in very late. We were supposed to stay in bed and keep quiet until our father got up. This was very difficult for us three kids to do. It seemed that we tried to play quietly, but we were not successful, and we laughed too much. It would start with my father telling us to shut up, then shut the fuck up, then get in your fucking corners. More than anything else in that house, I remember the time spent in our corners. We each had our assigned corners that we used as far back as I can remember. You had to be upright on your knees, with your nose touching the wall. We had wood floors with no carpeting, which was very difficult for our knees. My father would yell from time to time, "up on your fucking knees." My father would try and sneak up on us, and if we were not upright with our nose touching the wall, we would get the belt. If we were in the position that he required, to instill fear in us, the wall got the belt, which made a very impressive sound. The three of us could not see each other, but most of the time my brother and sister would scream and cry, and I could hear that belt. After a while, we were told that we could get up, and we knew that his rage was over. We were simply too noisy for our father, so this dance went on for many years.

When I was fourteen years old, we made a trip back to New Hampshire. That home that we had lived in, was then lived in by our uncle Bucky, my father's brother. We actually got to go in and see our old home. Without saying one word to each other, my brother, my sister, and I walked over to our previous corners and just stared at that wall. The hole that I picked in the pinewood wall over the years was still there, just filled in with something clear. All three of us, for many years, had knee problems, and my sister credits her knee replacements to the time spent in her corner.

Our father always desired to dominate us. One time, when I was about four years old, my father was wrestling with me. He was twisting my legs and arms and starting to get angry because I would not say uncle, and he was really hurting me. He kept saying, "say uncle," and I kept saying "no." I was really crying, and my mom walked in. My dad said to her that I would not say uncle. He finally let me go and got up. I was left laying on the floor, crying. I have no idea why I would not say uncle, but I did not give that fucking asshole the satisfaction that he was seeking. I very seldom gave up in life, even though it might have been painful.

Our father did not just reserve his rage for us. Sometimes my mom was the recipient of his anger. One time, I went into our parents' bedroom to look at a Daisy BB gun that belonged to our father. While I was inspecting the air rifle, I discharged a BB and shot off a piece of a glass lampshade on the ceiling. I heard our parents arguing, and they were bringing it to their bedroom where I was. I went and hid under the bed with the rifle, which is where I had found it anyway. Our father was screaming at our mom. I saw our father push mom against the wall, then throw her to the floor. While she was crying, he pinned her down and was screaming in her face. He was not hitting her, he was just rageful. I was crying, and crying out for them to stop fighting. Well, our father looked at me, and then it was my turn, which gave my mom time to slip away. He said that he would give me something to cry about. He did not beat me, he just vented his rage at me. The really cool thing is, that missing piece of glass was never brought up.

I recently spoke with my sister Debbie about our life in that home, and she reminded me that I almost lost my balls there. Debbie asked me what I had done to piss off our father so much. I was only about four or five years old for that one, too. I have no idea what I was thinking, but I took my father's pack of cigarettes. The cigarettes smelled so good to me, so I took out a cigarette and unwrapped the paper around the tobacco, and put the tobacco in a neat pile. I then took another cigarette and did the same thing. Eventually, I had all of the cigarettes unwrapped, and the tobacco neatly in a pile. While I was looking at, and smelling the tobacco, reality suddenly kicked in. I heard my father say, "Has anyone seen my cigarettes?"

I started to feel terrible horror, I froze there, looking at the pile of tobacco. Shit started to get worse - "Has anyone seen my fucking cigarettes, where are my fucking cigarettes?" I could hear my father getting closer to the enclosed front porch where the dismantled cigarettes and I were. As he was going through the house, and coming closer to the porch, his voice was becoming more desperate, and his mouth more profane. He came out to the porch and saw me and asked me if I saw his fucking cigarettes. I was just frozen there. He looked at me and then at that nice pile of tobacco, and the horror in his face was the worst that I have ever seen. I have no idea how I did it, but as he was recovering from his initial shock, I very quickly slipped past him and got into the house. Maybe I thought that someone would save me, but I hid behind a chair in the living room. This monster was after me, besides whatever the fuck came out of his mouth, he screamed that when he caught me, he was going to cut off my fucking balls. He threw that chair aside, and I made it to behind the couch. The couch was thrown aside very quickly, and I slipped past him again and ran down the hall to our parents' bedroom.

My father kept yelling that when he caught me, he was going to cut off my fucking balls. He was screaming at my mom, "Roberta, give me a fucking knife." He tried to reach me under the bed, but I scrambled to the other side. There were springs under the bed to support the mattress, which I held onto as he slid the bed with ease on the wood floor. He went to the side that I was on, but I moved to the other side. He slid the bed again, then he gave up on that idea. He threw the blankets and the mattress off the bed, all the while yelling, "Roberta, where is my fucking knife?" My father looked down at me, where I was shaking and hanging onto the springs. All of a sudden, my father snapped out of it and left the room. I got up and went to my room, and nobody said anything to me. Needless to say, I did not touch any cigarettes in my childhood again. As a matter of fact, I have never smoked one cigarette in my life. My mom never gave that asshole the knife either.

One incident in that home causes me much sadness and shame. I believe that I was also four years old at the time. We always held my brother's hand when we walked with him because he was very small. Because of a new water well that had been dug, there was a dirt pile behind our house. We took my brother's shoes and buried them in that pile of dirt. My brother would dig and find his shoes. We were all having fun, so I did not think that we were doing something bad. After doing this for a while, we could not find one shoe. We were in a panic, as they were new shoes. Debbie held one hand of our brother, and I held the other hand. We went to find our parents to tell our story and seek help to recover the other shoe. Our parents were coming out the door as we got there. They saw that one shoe was missing. Before we could say a word, our father grabbed our brother and started spanking him very hard. My sister and I were just frozen there, and we did not say one word to save our brother from him. Years later, after my breakdown, I actually spoke to my mom about this incident. I also, later in life, spoke to my older sister about this. I could not talk to my brother about it, because he died before my memory of it surfaced. I did not talk to my father about this either before he died. The many things that my brother did to hurt me during our lives, does not really bother me now. Not taking the blame myself, for something that he did not do, bothers me deeply to this day.

My father's dad lived right next door to us, and he was very nice to us kids. Our father and our grandfather argued a lot. We could go in and out of his house any time, we seemed to be of no bother to him. Our grandfather would take my brother and me digging for worms and fishing. Sometimes we would go fishing on a boat, and sometimes we would trek through the woods and mosquitos, and fish a large stream. When we brought the fish home, our father would usually clean and fry the fresh fish we caught.

When I was 8 years old, we had to leave our house. Our father and grandfather had a huge fight, and we were out. I recently asked my mom her recollection as to why we had to move, and she said that she was not sure. Before my father died, he started to tell me some of the things that he had done. My father claimed that he was given the business when our grandfather retired. Without our grandfather pushing our father, he did not take care of the business properly. After my breakdown, my father told me that he was more interested in fornicating with his customers then effectively managing the business. I do not know where the money went, but our main part supplier cut him off, and our grandfather wanted his tools back, and us out of his house.

We moved to an old farmhouse that had not been lived in for a while, and I heard that after we moved out, it was not lived in again. This house that we lived in was very close to our school. Sometimes we would walk, sometimes we would ride the bus.

I used to be afraid of snakes and tried to stay away from them. I could be 20 feet away, if I saw a snake curled up, I was terrified. One day when I was about 6 years old living in our first home, I hiked up a hill to pick wild Blueberries. I intended like I always do, to bring those Blueberries home, clean them, add milk and sugar, and enjoy them. The wild grass, maybe knee-high to me, covered most of the ground. And then I saw it, instant fear, I froze. The snake was slithering right in front of me, and then it stopped, inches away from me. Out of nowhere a calmness came over me. Without thinking, I reached down and I picked up that snake, and somehow I created a bond. In an instant, I was free of the fear of snakes. This farmhouse which we moved into had considerable amounts of overgrown brush, and wild grass. This was a perfect habitat for snakes to live in and a wonderful location to meet many of my new friends. I would pick up many snakes, cuddle them for a while, and release them. Some snakes I took a little longer to release. One day, I came home from school and I was greeted by my mom, who was in an elevated state of anxiety. My mom had placed a large towel under a door that entered the bedroom of my younger brother and myself. My mom was afraid that some of the snakes that were in my dresser drawers would come out and slither around our home. To her shock and dismay, my mom had learned of my collection while trying to put clean clothes inside my dresser.

An event happened which stopped me from picking up snakes for the next four years. One warm summer afternoon, my older sister, our babysitter, and I were outside in the front of that farmhouse. I saw a beautiful snake, I picked up that beautiful snake and I went to show it to my older sister. My sister was wearing a sleeveless shirt, and her back was towards me. As the snake and I got close to her, I called out her name, Debbie. As Debbie was turning around, somehow that snake crawled on her. The snake slithered onto her shoulder and across her back, under her shirt. The head of that snake poked out of her left arm sleeve, and the tail of that snake poked out of her right arm sleeve. Debbie was terrified, and I was a little shocked at what just happened. Debbie was running around our front yard screaming, with the snake bouncing around, affixed to her body. At first, the spectacle seemed humorous to me, and then I kicked into gear and removed that snake from Debbie. However, there were consequences for my action. I was to remain outdoors well into the evening, even after a thunder, lighting and rain storm moved in. I was also banned from any more contact with these friends of mine, the snakes.

At that farmhouse, my brother and I spent a lot of time together outdoors. One day while out playing, my brother and I threw a crab apple at a cow, and that cow chased us. This cow could not close the gap between her and us before we jumped over a stone wall to escape. This became a game, we would get close, toss crab apples, then easily go over a stone wall to escape from the cows. We repeated this many times until we ran out of crab apples. When the cows moved away, we moved to the apple tree to rearm ourselves with more crab apples. The cows slipped back in on us, and our escape path was blocked, so we climbed the apple tree. The cows decided to stay there and graze for a very long time. When we finally got down from the tree and got away, we did not play that game with the cows anymore. Actually, we later became friends with a boy whose parents owned a dairy farm and those cows. My brother and I were invited to hang around and play at this dairy farm. We would play in the hayloft, and we could watch the cows being milked. As the cows were being fed in an assembly line, to remove their waste as they were eating, there was a conveyor belt under them, quite efficient. You could go up to the cows with no problem - they were gentle creatures, and they did not seem to hold a grudge against us.

CHAPTER 2

Transitions

The first time that our father planned to commit suicide, he was taken to a special hospital to receive help. Sadly, our home became a little more peaceful while he was hospitalized. I remember going to Concord and seeing my father from the parking lot. We were not allowed in the hospital, so we stood down in the parking lot while our father waved to us from his room window.

After our father came back home to us, we moved to a small town named Pittsfield. Many people in this town were very poor, and there were many troubled kids there. I soon started to play with a little gang of boys. One day, a boy took out a slingshot and slung a small pebble at an old man. The pebble hit the old man in the head, and I saw his head snap forward. I was in shock, along with the sadness that I felt for that old man. These sick boys were all just laughing. Except for a bully that I once had to deal with, I never saw this kind of behavior from a kid before. I did not want to play with them anymore, so they started to bully me. They first started with verbal assaults, and I told them, fuck you, and flipped them off. Of course, they chased me, and most of the time I would get away. Three times I did get my ass kicked, but I also got in two good licks. The big boy of their group made the mistake of coming after me alone. There were so many rocks around me on the ground. I nailed that boy many, many times with rocks, and my brother and I were never bothered by those misguided assholes again.

In Pittsfield, we first lived in an apartment over a doughnut shop. We were no longer middle class, we were quite poor. You could receive money from finding and cashing in bottles, so my brother and I would look for bottles and cash them in from the store close to our home. One day while looking for bottles, the back of this store was open, and we could see crates of empty bottles. My brother and I helped ourselves to some bottles, and we later returned them to the front of the store for our deposit money. I should say that I was the older brother, therefore I was the responsible person for our little crime spree. With the money that we collected, we could go to the movies. At that time, about 1962, in that town, you could see two movies and get a piece of candy for 25 cents. Twice we went to the movies with the wealth from our bottle money. This was great until our money supply dried out.

My brother and I each had a toy rifle that looked like a Winchester Model 94 carbine. These toy rifles had toy bullets. The bullets had fake brass casings and fake lead. You put a cap on the base of the casing and pushed the fake lead into the spring-loaded casing. When you squeezed the trigger, the cap would fire, creating an explosion, and the fake lead would shoot out of the rifle. Pretty neat, we thought. When we made our second raid for bottles in the back of the store, we accidentally left one of the rifles there. I was not interested in going back for that rifle or asking for it to be returned to us. I did not think back then that I was committing a crime, it was just a dumb thing to do. I also think that the Lord helped teach me a lesson on that one, the rifle was worth more than the bottles.

When I was six years old, my brother, who was four and a half, and I, armed with a 22 rifle, would go off shooting on our own. Our father would buy ammo for us when we went to our grandparents' house, and we used our grandfather's 22 rifle. This was pretty neat until it was taken away from us. We did not shoot animals, mainly cans, until one day. There was an old abandoned one-room schoolhouse, very old, with a nice brick chimney. My brother and I systematically chipped away at those bricks, with that 22 rifle that our grandfather had loaned us. When our grandfather came home that day and drove past that old one-room schoolhouse, he immediately knew what had transpired. Once we got the right to shoot again, we were under adult supervision with all firearms. That mountain, where our grandparents lived, used to have a little community there, and the state of New Hampshire was considering preserving that old one-room schoolhouse.

I am not sure at what age I started shooting a rifle, but we shot rifles as far back as I can remember. One time, grandfather and uncle John were shooting a shotgun. I was about 6 years old, and grandfather asked me if I wanted to shoot it. I did, and I said yes. I squeezed off a shot, and ended up right on my ass, with my shoulder hurting like hell. They thought that it was funny, and asked me if I wanted to shoot it again. I did not shoot it again, nor did I fire a shotgun again, until I was an adult.

Our grandfather had an old car, that was used to haul wood. Someone cut out the doors, the trunk, most of the roof, most of the sides, rear, except part of the roof above the front seats. There was just a floor from the front seats back. My uncles would stack wood in that bare car, and sometimes my brother and I would ride in the back, and we would hold onto the piece of roof that had not been cut away. It was a blast. There were dirt roads through the woods. One day, as we were racing through the woods, with my brother and I holding on in the back, we went over a bump, and I flew out. I bounced down the road a bit but received no injuries. It was just more like an e-ticket ride at Disneyland. We would many times help our uncles stack the wood into the big woodshed that Grandpa, with the help of our uncles, built. I can still remember, and I absolutely loved, the smell of the wood as it seasoned in that woodshed.

When our uncle John would visit, he would almost always take me for walks with him. In the mountains near that farmhouse, I took many long walks with just my uncle. Uncle John was second only to grandma, as to the love I felt. Over the years, I would see uncle John, and we would still go on walks together.

Anyone who has visited the mountains of New Hampshire can understand the beauty. We loved being in that home in the Spring, Summer, Fall, or Winter. I loved being there in thunder and lightning storms, or snowstorms. I just loved being there. Being in that home with our grandmother, and the natural beauty around us, is the closest thing I can think of to Heaven on Earth. Except for the few drunken incidents with our grandfather, it was Heaven.

We had no money, so at 9 years old I tried to earn honest money. That winter, I knocked on doors as I lugged my snow shovel, and asked people if I could shovel the snow from their pathway. Not one person gave me a job.

I really do not know why but I thought it would be fun to play with bees. At eight years old and out walking, I ran into some boys who were friends of mine. These boys were throwing small stones at a beehive which was hanging from the back of an apple cider mill. From the safe distance they chose, they could not hit this beehive. From their location, I attempted to hit this beehive, but my aim was no better. I thought up this great idea. I would walk up and place a small stone in the single entrance of that cone shaped beehive. I was successful, however Three bees escaped and I was chased. These three bees pursued me for a while, definitely long enough for me to realize that it is best to leave these bees alone. Shortly after my cider mill incident, my brother and I hiked to an old abandoned sawmill. The woods were starting to reclaim this sawmill, and there were rusted out cars, which had beehives in them. At this sawmill, there were spear-like sticks laying around on the ground. I decided to throw one through the car back window with the missing glass, towards the hive. As predicted Bees flew out to chase me, as I ran. These bees were a different type of a bee, compared to the bees, which I had trouble with before. These bees were better tempered, and they did not chase me as far. I played this game with the bees until justice decided to step in. On what turned out to be my last attempt at throwing a spear, I missed my mark, and part of that spear stuck out of the car. As I ran, I got snagged on this spear, which slowed me down, and the bees taught me a lesson.

Not long after this saw mill experience, my last major encounter with Bees, was near our grandparents' home. My younger sister Alberta, my brother and I were walking over a bridge which crossed a stream. This stream had dried out, for lack of rain that summer. Below the bridge, on the dried stream bed, my brother noticed a three-pronged spear tip and he wanted it. Unbeknownst to me, I had stepped on an underground bees nest, while walking down the embankment to retrieve that spear tip. As I stood up from picking up that spear tip, I was swarmed with bees. I ran up the embankment, picked up my much younger sister, then my brother and I ran to our grandparents' home. My sister Alberta received no stings, my brother had 5 stings on one foot which swelled up very badly. I brought back to my grandmother's house two or three bees still inside of my shirt. For my effort, I received 28 Bee stings. This did not feel good, but other than a bit of pain, I did not display any allergic reactions. Unlike the other two times, I had not tried to antagonize these bees. I did receive some punishment with my last set of bees, but maybe karma figured I needed a little more education. Since then, I have never ever antagonized any bees. As a matter of fact, I love bees, and, of course, I have a great deal of respect for them.

We left that apartment in Pittsfield and moved into a house a little out of town, at the bottom of a hill. My parents rented a house, and this was much better for my brother and me. Now that I think about it, we did not have a corner in that house to kneel in, with our noses touching the walls, nor did we have a corner in that apartment. There was a stream that ran between our home and our neighbor's home. There was a river to fish, maybe one-half mile away, and there were woods to hike through. My brother and I did a lot of hiking and fishing there. Our father planted a garden in the back pasture, and I drew water from the stream each day to water the garden. I built a small treehouse there, and my brother and I built a small fort. I used to play marbles a lot for a few years. I won a lot of marbles, I had an oatmeal box of marbles, and many bags full of marbles. My sister and my brother loved marbles also, but they did not have many. One day, we sat down and I split the marbles up three ways, a third for each of us. Our father walked in and asked what I was doing. He got angry and told my sister and brother to give me back my marbles. Their hearts were broken, and I was very sad. I do not think that I played marbles ever again, and I have no idea as to what happened to those marbles.

We had a babysitter watching us and she asked me to go get my brother and older sister who were playing at our neighbor's home. I do not know what I was thinking, but I started playing with everyone, and I forgot what I was there for. Time went by, then I remembered what I was supposed to do, and we got home late. The babysitter was upset, and when our parents got home, she relayed this to them. Our father came into the room where my brother and I were and started yelling at me. I started to explain that I got caught up in playing. In a rage, our father grabbed my brother and me by the throat. I thought that I would blackout, but my brother actually did blackout. Our father snapped out of it, and he let us go, and my brother fell to the floor. Our father did not even check to see if my brother was okay, he just left that room.

It was shortly after this that our father left us. Our mom received some money from the government, but it did not go directly to her. The money went to the people who rented the house to us. Those same people owned a grocery store in town, so we received our weekly food directly from them. My mom never received any cash, so we lost our phone service. I have no idea how we got our electricity covered. After our father left, my older sister and brother would fight a lot. After our father left was the first time that my brother attacked me. I started to stay away from home more and kept to myself. We did not fish or go on hikes together any longer. I would walk through the woods by myself, and I would walk up the hill into town. I would walk to a park in town, and there were always older men there playing chess. I would lay on a concrete and stone wall that was close to them, and I would watch them play their chess games. I would just watch them which was very peaceful. The men never said one word to me, they just smiled and kept playing chess. From my world, I had a safe respite.

I was walking into town shortly after our father left us, and our father drove by. He saw me and picked me up. My father drove me into town and gave me 50 cents, which was a lot of money back then. My father told me that I was the man of the house now, great for a 9-year-old. No hugs, no I love you, although, maybe the 50 cents was his way of giving me love. I did not see our father again until we caught up with him in California. I have talked to my older sister about our youth in New Hampshire. Neither of us ever remember receiving a hug or being told that we were loved, except at our grandmother's home. We were not told that we were loved, but we got many hugs, and we knew that we were loved by our grandmother.

My mom's parents lived at 99 Reed Road, in Alton, New Hampshire. Their home was built in the 1850s and was very rustic. When we got older, our grandfather added a bathroom and a bedroom to their house. Before the addition, they had a two-hole outhouse, close to the back door. During the winter you would bundle up, and take care of business quickly. During the summer you would be armed with fly swatters. Funny thing, I can still envision the crap pile over the years, growing closer to our seats. As I am typing this, I am wondering about something. Our outhouse was very close to our well that we drew our water from. Did we contaminate our water supply? Our grandmother would bathe us in a small portable tub. Our grandfather would have loaded rifles at some of the windows, in case a deer might happen by. In or out of deer season did not much matter to our grandfather. I would sometimes go into the detached garage and see a deer hanging there. My older sister and I, then later my brother, would stay at that home for about two or three weekends every month for many years. Sometimes we would stay there for a week at a time. Our grandmother was so unbelievably kind to us. She never once raised her voice to us, and we never would do anything to hurt her feelings. For a while, we had a neighbor up the road about a quarter of a mile, where there were two other children that we would play with. Their father was very abusive, many times we could hear their screams as they were being beaten. Sometimes when the brother and sister would come play with us, the boy would drop his pants, and show us the welts on his butt, and the back of his legs. Their house suddenly burnt down, and we lost our only other playmates who lived close by.

Our grandmother had many toys for us to play with in her house, and we also loved the outdoors on their mountain. There was a wood-burning stove to cook with, and a potbelly stove upstairs for heat. The downstairs was heated with a fireplace, and in the winter you were pretty damn cold until the fireplace got going. There was a Helms truck that would come up our road on Saturdays, just for their house, that was really a cool treat. On Saturday nights there was wrestling. Our grandmother and us kids would watch wrestling, eat saltine crackers with the lights out, and the fire going. Uncle Jimmy would many times come over and stay with us for the weekend. Many times uncle John would come to visit. Uncle Paul would visit sometimes too. If any of the uncles stayed there, my brother and I would sleep in the same bed with an uncle. Until the addition was built, the three rooms were divided by hanging blankets on a rope, which acted as walls. The rooms were divided as the grandparents' room, the girls' room, and the boys' room. We would many times experience bats flying around in that room at night. The bats did not seem to bother my brother and me, but my sister and aunt were not happy with them at all. The upstairs had a tall A-frame ceiling with open beams that I always seemed to count as I lay there, like counting sheep, to fall asleep.

Our grandfather was absent much of the time, and once in a while, he tried to act mean, but he never hurt us. Our grandfather would say that we are to be seen, but not heard. When our grandfather came home drunk, that really sucked. He did not yell at, or hurt us, but he would yell at, and push our grandmother around. One time, he was so drunk and angry, he pushed our grandmother's head through the living room door. When our grandfather went upstairs, my sister and I tried to comfort our grandmother as she was crying. We had to comfort our grandmother a few times because of our grandfather's drunken rage.

After we moved to Pittsfield, for a while our father worked for a company delivering heating oil. Our father had a childhood friend named Roger Lumbra. Roger and his wife Dottie had previously moved to Los Angeles, California, from Laconia, New Hampshire. Without our knowledge, our father left New Hampshire and moved to Los Angeles, California, where he moved in with Roger and Dottie. Once he got established, he wrote to our mom, and invited us to move to California, and be together again as a family. On a night with a severe winter storm in Boston, Massachusetts, we boarded a plane with our older sister screaming, so that all of New England could hear her. We left our heaven in the mountains forever as children, and we touched down in Los Angeles, California, where dark clouds and hell were waiting to receive us. I am thinking that the reason for my older sister's primal scream is that she had foreseen the future, but no one would listen. My older sister was just under eleven years old, my younger brother was eight years old, my youngest sister was three years old, and I was just under ten years old.

CHAPTER 3

The Nightmare Begins

From the air, as we were nearing the Los Angeles airport, what we were seeing was unbelievable to us. So many lights, so many cars. The airport, the stores, the freeways, we had never seen anything like this before. We first lived in an apartment in Los Angeles, near Macarthur Park. My brother and I were free to roam the streets of Los Angeles, just like we were in a small town or the mountains in New Hampshire. As we were walking the streets of Los Angeles, we were never bothered by anyone. Much of our time was spent at Macarthur Park. We just lived there for a short time, before we moved to Argyle Street in Hollywood. That was an interesting street to live on, as we had everything: drugs, transvestites, hookers, hillbillies. We had a transvestite living right next to us who was very kind to us children. It was sad when the police took him away, and we never saw him again. We had two ladies who were gay, and they were incredibly nice to us. I would also play chess with one of those ladies. We had two families from the hills of West Virginia who would sometimes quarrel. During one disagreement, they each had a rifle sticking out of their window, pointed towards the other.

There was a man named Tim who drank a lot, who I also played chess with. One night, Tim came outside drunk and naked, and he fell flat on his face. Tim tried to crawl into the home of the two gay ladies which was quite a scene. Tim was taken to the hospital to get fixed up, and he was fine. He would not always be nice to me when we played chess. Sometimes I would goof off with some of the other kids that lived there, while we were playing chess together, and he was not happy about that. He would take out his frustration by twisting my ankle. Tim and my father did not get along well, which was a bit stressful. Later, I think Tim's attitude caught up with him, he was found dead up the street from where we lived, a victim of murder with a bullet to the head and a knife that was still stuck in his throat. Until my father found out and put a stop to it, I played poker with some adults that lived near us. Many times you could turn on the news and see our street where we lived, and we were called the hottest place in town.

My brother and I would sometimes spend time walking Hollywood Blvd. Many times, my brother and I would walk to Griffith Park. It was not like the woods in New Hampshire, but it had some open space. We did earn our corners again, and my brother still received spankings. My brother was really starting to change, and he was lashing out at me. He went off on another boy, and almost took out that boy's eye. I tried to talk to my parents about this, but I would only get scolded. I started to want to be alone again. I started to walk alone, and I would skateboard alone.

#

Before I started junior high school, we moved to a two-bedroom home on Cartwright Ave in North Hollywood. Our parents had one room, and us four kids had another room. There was a Boy Scout troop down the street from us, at a church, which I checked out. After two or three visits, I saw a man there give a speech. He was in full military uniform, tall, with a chest full of medals. He was a jet fighter pilot, and he had fascinating stories about flying a fighter jet. He had seen combat, and he was able to draw you into some of his missions. This man, John Dark, was going to become an assistant boy scoutmaster. I ended up joining troop three in North Hollywood, California. Just like in New Hampshire, I would be able to spend time outdoors. We would hike, camp, learn first aid, tie knots, cook outdoors, learn archery, shoot rifles, just to name a few things. When we were hiking together, we learned to sing together. When we were camping, we were a team. We all knew how to set up our campsites and cook. At night, we would sing songs, do skits, and tell stories. We would pray together; this was a wonderful time.

I signed up for the silver knapsack, which was a one-week hiking and camping trip. John Dark was the only adult that would be on this hiking and camping trip. Every morning I was the first person awake. I thought that it was strange, John Dark and another boy were sleeping in the same sleeping bag together. John said that it was cold in the middle of the night and that we all might consider doubling up together. None of us other boys doubled up, except this boy and John Dark. One of those nights, we camped at Twin Lakes. The lake water was very cold, but another boy and I managed to take a swim. We hit a lot of rain, but we built an effective roof over our camping area.

One morning, while the sun was just starting to show itself, I grabbed my soap, my plastic soap box and my face towel to wash up. About 300 yards from us was a stream. At this stream was a little waterfall, maybe three feet tall, this was the area which I chose to wash up. As I was washing my face, I clearly heard the sound of a rattle from a rattlesnake. I looked up and I was eyeball to eyeball, looking directly at a curled up rattlesnake. I jumped backward, and I took off. I was so impressed with that rattlesnake that I did not return for my soap, soapbox, or washcloth. From that incident, I learned a new healthy fear of snakes. Later, I came to believe that this rattlesnake was of no danger to me. It was cold, it knew that I was no threat to it. I came to believe that I was not warned of danger from that snake, but of danger which lurked back at our camp. I was warned but I did not listen.

On our next to the last day, we had a long hike under a steady downpour. We were wearing our ponchos, but the trail was very wet. We came across a couple who had set up quite a campsite. They had their sleeping tent and another tent that was their kitchen. Their kitchen tent had three sides, with a makeshift kitchen table. Their food was stored in sealed containers, which were in a tree, to keep away from the bears. We hung out with them for a couple of hours, and they served us coffee. This was the first time in my life that I drank coffee. With the cold and rain, that cup of coffee was a blessing. The couple were mining Tungsten, and they had a few bags with $20.00 marked on the outside of each bag. Soon we were on our way, and we left our gracious hosts.

#

By the mid-90s, because of my many physical and emotional issues, I received various tests from three different doctors. The last doctor, Dr. Baker, told me in December 1996 that I would not live to see 1998. I remember thinking, 'that long?' The thought of death did not bother me in the slightest. I was ready, I was going home. I went about my daily routine, just as before. I felt even God thought my life was near its end, so God had another idea. I needed a bit more pain before I died. In January 1997, the only person that I know of in this world who could have such an incredible emotional impact on me, Sally, called my parents. After more than 25 years of never seeing or thinking of her, she called. Just to ensure that the impact of her call would have the most extreme impact on me, she said that "our children are okay." After having absolutely no memory of any rape, or molestation, or for that matter, much of any of my youth, one single phone call forever altered my life. Firstly, the childhood memories that I had crammed deep inside of me, came flooding out. Secondly, the thought that I would have abandoned children was almost more than I could deal with. In my youth, Sally tried to tell me that her twin boys were mine. The problem with this was that I had no idea how my sperm could have entered her. Even though my mind could figure this out, I was thinking after so many years, what woman would still tell this story? Maybe just Sally and me sitting on the couch together was an escape for her also. I believe the thought of those boys, with the memories flowing out of me, completely emotionally broke me within three days. I had a complete and utter breakdown.

Those incredible memories spilling out of me were like a broken bag of marbles. I just could not catch them, and shove them back in my bag fast enough. I gave up and started crying, and crying, and crying. I could be at work for maybe a half-hour, then I had to go for a walk and cry. With zero appetite, I forced myself to eat a can of tuna and an apple a day. I lost so much weight, and you could rule out sleep. I wrote a letter to my parents, and I told them the story and asked them to help find me a therapist, but it had to be a woman. I did not want to talk about this shit to another man. The unbelievable shame that I was feeling was almost unbearable. I could not believe the events of my childhood, how long it lasted, and my total inability to stop what was happening to me. I still struggle with this shame at 64 years of age. I thought that my mind was making this shit up. The interesting thing is that within a few months, I understood the gift that God had given me. Tremendous amounts of buried stress was pouring out of my body, and all of my health symptoms simply disappeared. I am glad that the Lord has a sense of humor because, for the first time in my life, I cursed God plenty. The memories that returned were horrific.

#

One of the first memories to return was about John Dark being friends with a family who owned a painting company, called ABC Painting. They had internal spray booths, and they painted parts for various companies. A few families were invited to their property in the mountains for the weekend. My mom, dad, my older sister Debbie, and I went from our family. I do not remember where my brother and my younger sister were that weekend.

The families met at the bottom of the mountain, and somehow some of us kids rode the rest of the way in the back of a camper. I think that there were about six of us kids, in the back of this camper. One of those six was a very pretty girl, my age. I was awestruck with her, and it was very difficult keeping my eyes off of her. I was too shy to talk, but it was very difficult for me to keep my eyes off her to look away. Most of us kids slept in sleeping bags on the ground. I am not sure where the parents slept. That girl and I think two other girls, slept maybe 20 to 30 feet from me. During the night, John Dark, who was also there for the weekend, crawled into my sleeping bag and sodomized me, right there. I was crying so bad inside of me, but I tried not to make any noise. I was listening for any noise from the girls, but I did not hear one sound from them. When John Dark finished, I did not get up to go to the outhouse. I just lay there all night, with what he put in me.

The next morning, I left camp and went off by myself. I was very depressed, and I stayed away most of the day. When I returned, this pretty girl was waiting for me. She told me that they had to leave, and she took my hand and we walked for a little while. We did not really talk, we mainly walked a bit; she then gave me a hug and said goodbye to me. I feel that this girl knew what had happened to me, 20 to 30 feet away from her. I also feel that this girl knew what something like this feels like. Either way, I never saw that pretty girl again.

Shortly after that hiking and camping trip, John Dark was to form his own patrol. I was asked by John to be the patrol leader. I became the patrol leader of the Eagle patrol. There was an upcoming Jamboree, about 30 days away. We had all new boy scouts in our new patrol, who possessed no skills needed for our upcoming event. These boys came to our house almost every day so I could teach these skills to everyone. We practiced, practiced, practiced, starting a fire without matches, setting up our campsite, tying knots, etc. With this continuous training, we ended up receiving the most points in that Jamboree. John Dark was considered to be a hero for this fantastic feat. I have since learned, during my quest to stop John Dark, that it is quite possible that many boys from that Eagle patrol over time were sexually molested by John Dark. Besides our patrol, John Dark molested two Erics, Mark, James, and maybe Hank and George from Troop Three in North Hollywood. John Dark was like an old bull on the hill. An old bull and a young bull were standing on a hill overlooking cows down in the pasture. The young bull says, let's run down and get us one of them cows. The old bull says, let's mosey down and get all of them cows. That impressive uniform and speech by John Dark was his hunting uniform, and we were the hunted.

John became aware that I played chess, and eventually he started to visit our home to play games of chess with me. John Dark was the first person in my young life that I lost a game of chess to. Playing chess with an adult man was not a new experience for me, so this did not raise any red flags for anyone in our family. John was always a gentleman to my parents, and to me. It is so fucking amazing to me, that he could so brazenly groom me for his evil acts, in front of everyone in our home, with absolutely no fucking remorse. John ultimately asked, and received permission from my mom, for me to go to his home to play chess. I was picked up by John, and driven to his apartment in North Hollywood. He lived in a one-bedroom apartment with very little furniture, and as I would later see, in his bedroom, there was a small bed.

\#

As I grew older, I started to become more attracted to girls, especially this one girl. I was daydreaming about the day that I could start dating. I don't remember thinking about kissing, and I knew almost nothing of sex. I had not been sexually stimulated or had an orgasm, but I was thinking of girls. I think that as your body matures, there is a natural way of becoming sexually aware. Probably a healthy way that nature planned. If a wrong thing happens, like childhood sexual molestation, you are forever robbed of this beauty.

\#

When we arrived at John's apartment, the chessboard was set up and ready to play. We almost immediately started to play a game of chess; everything was innocent at this point. Then he started putting his arm around me, and he started talking to me about things that he nor anyone else had ever talked to me about before. I was getting very uncomfortable. I wanted to go home, and I tried to get up, but he had a very firm hold on me. He was going between calmly talking to me, and getting frustrated with me. My brain was starting to get foggy, and he was becoming more aggressive. He was talking about an orgasm, I did not understand what he was talking about. He wanted to have sex with me. I was trying to figure out how a man has sex with another man. I was maybe 5 feet tall, he was over 6 feet tall, he had such a strong grip on me, that it was difficult for me to breathe. I was starting to hyperventilate, I was extremely confused, my mind was going crazy, what in the fuck was happening? He was trying to calm me down, but he was also very forceful. I felt that I was going to die if he did not get what he wanted. But what did he want? I was trying to figure this out. I started to tell myself, how bad could this be. I did not know what he wanted to do to me, but I soon found out. I think that I went into some kind of shock, and I became numb.

He took me into his bedroom, he removed my clothes, he placed me face down on his bed. This is where reality sunk in, and I learned what the plan really was. He started to enter me, and because I was starting to scream, he covered my mouth. I grabbed onto his metal bedpost, and I tried to squirm away. Soon it was over, and I was numb. I was totally wasted, I was broken, absolutely fucking broken. I slowly started to dress, as he called me a sissy. He took me home, dropped me off, and he somehow knew that I would never open my mouth. He was a seasoned child molester, that had perfected this many times before. He came into my parents' home, he made friends with everyone, took their son to his home with their permission, and he fucking raped me. He took me back to the home that welcomed him with open arms, and dropped me off, all the time knowing that he could do this with impunity. How in the fuck does a human mind develop this type of evil skill? My family had become so disarmed by his grooming that they did not notice, one child left with John Dark and another child returned home. Little Raymond went into John Dark's apartment, but he never came out.

#

I have a picture of my Mom, Dad, and me in my boy scout uniform. My Mom is just under five feet tall, and I was shorter than her. When I look at that picture, I wonder how anyone could do what John Dark did to me. It does not take thinking of the past, or hearing other stories of child molestation, to bring the sorrow in me to the surface. Below are summaries of two articles that I have read, that tap into the feeling of when I was raped and repeatedly molested by John Dark.

On a cattle ranch in Montana, a young bull was about to be castrated. The bull was prancing around full of energy, vitality, and feeling strong in the world. They roped this young bull, and drove him to the ground, when on the ground they severed his balls. They threw his cut-off balls to a dog who ate them. I think they then cauterized his wound. When they let the bull up, he staggered to his feet, his eyes glazed and his tongue hanging out. In an instant, his energy, vitality, and zest for life were forever gone.

Probably the best light cavalry in the world was the Comanche Indian. They had a very unique way to break a wild horse. They would lasso a wild horse, tighten the noose so it could not breathe, and then they would drive that horse to the ground. The horse would desperately fight to breathe, but just before this horse was about to die, they would loosen the noose, stroke the horse around the neck, head, and blow air into its nostrils. After they let the horse up, the horse was ready to be ridden.

A master child molester will be the one that breaks and soothes the child. The child is then at the mercy of the child molester. The child molester has no mercy, they just have this strong need that is evil and uncontrollable. A child molester will need the right family dynamics for this to work, but a seasoned child molester has long figured this out. I actually discussed this with John Dark in one of our sting operations. I asked John Dark while it was being recorded by the L.A.P.D., how he knew that he could meet a young boy, do the things that he did, and the boy would tell no one. John Dark replied that he just knew. John Dark knew how to break a child, just like the Comanche Indian knew how to break a wild horse.

There are many articles on the internet from studies performed, which claim that if you have been victimized once, you have a very high chance of being victimized again. I think that we are vibrating at a level that says, victim. I also believe that you are already broken, therefore you do not need to be groomed, you are easy prey.

#

I did not think of that girl I thought I liked, or of holding her hand, or walking together to class, or home, or anywhere. As a matter of fact, I do not know if I ever thought of her again. I did not think of much for a very long time. I just wanted to be alone and crawl into my internal box. Nobody asked me if I was ok, was anything wrong, not one single person. I think that I was in a living coma, nothing in my life had prepared me for that moment. Nothing ever happened to me before. I slept many times with my uncles, and they never did anything to prepare me for this. Nobody ever, ever, did anything like this to me before, that would have made me aware of this terrible possibility.

Sometime later, maybe a week or so, John Dark came by and wanted to talk with me. He found me alone somewhere, and he was the motherfucker who tried to soothe me. I cannot believe this, he was the asshole to comfort me. That asshole somehow knew that I was broken, he just needed a little more finishing touches on me, to ensure that he would be able to molest me for about three more years, and right under the noses of everyone around me.

Funny, many times he would pick me up like a date, take me to play miniature golf, then to his place, where he would orally copulate, then sodomize me. I would close my eyes and pretend in my mind that I was with a girl, but being sodomized snaps you out of that quickly. I wanted it to end faster so I trained myself to have an orgasm quickly, which hurt me later in life. After I had an orgasm, I would fall into a deep depression. Even today, I will fall into a little depression after I orgasm. I became dysfunctional, I could barely have an erection, or not at all. There was a lady in her forties, living in an apartment next to John Dark. John borrowed a vibrator from her, and she wanted to share me with John. That lady would look at me and just smile. I was flushed with shame, and I turned around and walked into John Dark's apartment.

At some point, John Dark was quietly asked to leave the Boy Scouts. I do not know the details, no one talked to me about it. My father was an assistant scoutmaster, and he did not talk to me. I did not even talk to John Dark about this. I did not see him for a while, then he started coming around our home again.

I stayed in the Boy Scouts for a while after John Dark was gone, but I was starting to change more, I was much more serious. The boy who had been the troop leader, the same boy who doubled up with John Dark on the hiking and camping trip, stepped down. I would become the new troop leader. This did not last too long. One night, we had a visit from a past boy scout, who at one time had been this troop's leader. This boy would be the honorary troop leader for the night. All of the boy scouts were lined up outdoors. This honorary troop leader saw a girl in the parking lot near us. The boy ordered all of the scouts to run across the street, to go after this girl. Everyone except me ran after that girl. I unsuccessfully tried to call everyone back. Soon I became angry. I was arguing with one boy who was difficult to get back when I snapped. I started to choke the boy, but luckily my father who was there broke it up. I was shocked at myself, I had never acted out like this before. My father took me home, then I immediately quit the Boy Scouts. I would never again go back to Troop Three of North Hollywood.

CHAPTER 4

Coping with Agony

I started to pull away from my friends, and I became very quiet. I was pulling myself deeper, and deeper into my body. I was very much trying to shut the world out. I walked around aimlessly, I heard music but no words. At school, I did not want to speak in class. My grades were failing, which was causing me problems. I did not talk to anybody on our bus rides to and from school. One day, an older boy started to bother me on a bus ride home. I got off the bus early and he followed me. I tried to go into a store, but he grabbed me in the parking lot, and he wanted me to give him a blow job, right there during the day in this public parking lot. I was so scared again, and I said okay. When he started to undo his pants, I ran away. I ran down the middle of the fucking street, with all of the cars, and that asshole did not follow me.

I guess by that time, I had some kind of victim stamped on my forehead.

After that, I would not ride the bus anymore. I started to walk home. It took me a while to walk home, so I started to run partway. I started to run more and more, and the bus would pass me up. I started to see how far I could get before the bus would pass me up. The books were difficult to run with, so before I left school, I would place my books in my school locker. Eventually, I would be able to beat the bus to our bus stop. When I would finally have the ability to beat the bus to our bus stop, a girl would carry my books on the bus for me. I would be at the bus stop waiting for her, and this nice girl would return my books to me.

When I ran I was feeling better, I did not want to talk to people, but I felt better. Soon I started to do more exercises, pushups, sit-ups, chin-ups. I got so that I could climb the ropes in school like a monkey. I was not really good in a sprint, but I could run really far.

One day, Mom got us a heavy bag; she does not remember why she bought that. As far as I am concerned, this heavy bag was a gift from God. When I would punch the bag, I felt good, and if I punched it enough, I would sleep really well. I soon joined the Ryo Dojo in North Hollywood, and I learned a little bit of Kempo. I always felt better working out by myself, so I was not serious about the Dojo. I set myself a program, each set of punches was 100 punches, and kicks were 100 kicks, and a combination of punches and kicks was 100, on the heavy bag. I worked myself up to 30 sets of punches, 20 sets of kicks, and 10 sets of combinations, every single day, no days off, for over 3 years. I had to wrap myself in bandages because I bled a lot, I was in a rage while on that bag. Off from the bag, I was kind and mellow. Soon, I added weights to my ankles, I would run and kick like this. I created my own Katas and pretended that many people were attacking me at the same time. I went at the bag with a vengeance, it was my enemy and my friend. My father asked me how come I worked out so hard, and I claimed that I could not help it.

My life was so sad for me, and I also had to deal with my brother's rage. Many times he tried to attack me. He had already cut up a live cat and tried to gouge out a boy's eye. This shit was a challenge. My brother was not doing well, attacking me, so he told some people that we knew that while I slept, he would beat me with a baseball bat. This was a big concern for me, so I put a lot of effort into making sure that my brother was not angry before we went to sleep. I had this stupid idea that a pillow might soften the blow of the bat, so I would sleep with a pillow over my head. I also figured out that if I hugged a pillow, it would calm me down and make it easier to sleep. At 64 years old, about the beginning of December 2018, I quit hugging a pillow and having night-mares. I absolutely believe that it is because of writing down my story, that my need to hug a pillow disappeared. I also became ultra-sensitive while I slept, and it became dangerous for someone to try and wake me up. My older sister would use a broom handle as a tool to poke me, so I would wake up, and she would be out of the danger area.

#

On one occasion, my older sister and I were riding with John Dark in his 1964 Ford Ranchero. We were going on a camping trip, I think near Big Bear Lake. On the trip up there, I sat between John Dark and my older sister. It was dark outside and John Dark turned off the inside lights so it was also dark inside the vehicle. John Dark took my penis out of my pants and started to play with me. I think my sister was pretending to be asleep, and I cannot describe the deep emotional pain and shame that I was feeling. I could not get an erection, and John Dark was being very forceful. This became very painful and I ended up with three areas where the skin was rubbed off from my penis. It took a little time before it healed enough so that it was not painful to urinate. I cannot wrap my head around how a person like me could not stop this. I was not kidnapped, I did not have to physically escape, so what happened to my mind? I was in a prison that had no bars, no chains, no doors. I so badly did not want to do this, so what the fuck happened? I have spoken to many victims of this type of crime, and they feel the same way I do. We completely lost all our power, and these motherfuckers like John Dark know and gloat about this type of evil power which they have mastered.

#

As I write this, I am wondering, why could I not tell someone? Why is it that almost all of us victims will not tell anybody? Is there some kind of filter in society that stops this? Why could I not go to the police? Right now, I do not really fucking know. Whatever the fuck it is, most child molesters know this. Why did no one from the Boy Scouts turn him into the police? The Boy Scouts asked John Dark to leave, and the scoutmaster's son was molested by John Dark. My father was an assistant scoutmaster, why did he do nothing? Why did no one in my family know that something terrible happened to me, or my brother? Actually, our neighbor, Dale and his family, knew what was happening to me. They had found out through their Mormon church that John Dark was a pedophile. Why did they not try and help? One of their sons called me gay. That asshole became a rather famous person, and he dropped out of the limelight because of his own sex scandal. I do not know how that asshole managed to stay out of jail.

Another victim that I knew, who I believe was in a foster home, was being molested by an older boy in that home. He told me that on this one occasion after he was sodomized, they had to go downstairs for dinner. They were all sitting around the dinner table, eating and laughing, while he sat there in an internal rage. He asked me why could they be so happy, while his life was being destroyed? It would have been so easy for a few of us boys to walk into the police station, which was close to our home, and stop John Dark forever. The Boy Scouts or the Mormon Church could have ended this so easily. This is such a big disease in this country in large part to secrecy. I believe that shame is a big factor but not the biggest. I can now look shame in the eye, and say fuck you. It is the pain, the severe emotional pain. If we talk, we will feel this pain, which goes all the way to the soul.

I was really, really suffering in junior high school. During a break or lunch, I would just walk around, I could not sit, I could not talk to anyone. I did not have one single friend, I talked to almost no one. I know that girls were attracted to me, but I could not talk to them, except to the one girl who carried my books on the bus. This girl was very nice to me, but I never saw her except at school, and mainly at the bus. I could not speak up in class when the teacher would ask me a question, sometimes no words would come out. It was believed that I could not read, so I was sent to a special reading class. In this class, you would read a story, then take a test. That class was so simple, I read fast and retained what I read. The teacher thought I was smart, and when she looked at me, I could see the sadness in her eyes. She told me there was nothing wrong with my reading, and that I could stay in her class. I do not know if I ever said anything to her, but I would just read, take my tests, and I did not have to talk to anyone. I really believe that the teacher knew that I was traumatized.

John Dark would come many times to our house to have coffee with my mom. He was milking her for all it was worth. He just needed to ensure unfettered access to her children. By tending to our mom's emotional needs, this would help ensure his desires were met. It has been said in the family, that both my mom and dad were victims themselves of this same type of abuse. If the family stories are true, then this is one very sad story. I also feel so sad for my parents, mainly my mom, who in reality did the best she could with us children. My mom was concerned with her children, but she did not have any skills to understand friends from foe. My mom, just like so many, many other mothers and fathers, was no match for the evil mastery of a man like John Dark. We are all victims of people like John Dark. Until we get well educated and organized, good people will not have effective tools to help prevent these types of crimes. As we seek to find the good in people, do we fail to see the evil? My grades dropped badly, and my depression was so deep. Unknown to my mom, she had voiced her concerns to the same man who was sexually molesting her children.

This one day, John Dark and my mom were talking to me like two concerned parents. My mom was concerned, John Dark was just acting his evil part. My mom could not have had this discussion with my father, her and me. Our father would not have taken the time. My mom wanted to know what was happening to me. Why was I so sad, why was I failing in school, did I need help. I remember saying to them that the classes were easy, I just did not care. I remember telling them to pick one class, any class, and I would receive an A on every test until I finished that semester. They picked history class. For the rest of the semester, I did not get one single wrong answer on every test that I took in that class. I remember the teacher trying to figure out how I was cheating. I was not cheating, which he finally realized. Of course, except for that class, reading, and PE, I did not give a damn.

Our mom was also vulnerable to a man like John Dark. She had four children, and a husband who showed little concern for his children. John Dark seemed to be the knight in shining armor, who spent a considerable amount of time drinking coffee and talking to her. He helped himself to her two sons while she tried to keep her family together. My mom's relationship with my older sister was very strained. My father liked to look at my older sister, and not in a fatherly way. This did not get past our mom who was extremely critical of the clothes that Debbie wore. I am sure that our mom was concerned about our father. After all, it is said that my mom was a victim of sexual molestation from her own father. My father later in life said to me, my sister Debbie had a fucking beautiful body at the age of twelve. My father also told me that on our trip back to New Hampshire, his brother, our uncle Bucky, asked him, if he was fucking her yet, meaning my sister.

On another occasion, John Dark desired two boys at the same time, so he took that very boy from the silver knapsack and me to his sister's house on Kagel Canyon, a favorite location for John Dark. Like always, if his sister Marla was home, she would leave her house for a while. Like always, Marla would look at me and never say a word. John liked to undress his boys. I do not remember if we undressed or John

Dark undressed us on this day. John Dark performed a sex act on both of us, and the other boy was sodomized. I do not believe that this boy or I said one word to each other, and we never, ever talked about what happened. This boy and I lived two homes away from each other, which was very convenient for the motherfucker, John Dark. His mom would also have coffee with John Dark, then he would go back and forth between homes for a refill of coffee.

I had no one to talk to about what John Dark was doing to me, so for some stupid reason, I tried to talk to John. I told John that I did not want to do this anymore, I liked girls. John made a deal with me. John would introduce me to a girl, and he would keep doing to me what he had been doing. John brought me to the Gorman's home, where I met a girl named Sally. Sally was a very pretty girl, and it appeared that we were attracted to each other. This feeling did not get past John Dark. Week after week, John would take me to their house and all I did was sit on a couch with Sally while we did almost no talking. I just needed a little time with Sally, just a little time for me to leave my life, and feel the comfort of sitting with her. This was like some kind of drug that melted my body. I am not sure what Sally got out of this, but she had some kind of healing effect on me. Soon, John would show back up, we would then go to his home where he would do his thing, and then return me home. Once at home, I would sit on our one toilet, while his semen would noisily exit my body. This was a very slow agonizing death to endure, for I am quite sure that every single sound was heard by everyone in our small home.

After John Dark was finished, a deep depression would set in, and I would slowly dress. As John Dark would drive me home, I was usually in some type of coma. My eyes were open, I could see, but I could not talk. John Dark was driving and up ahead I could see a dog lying in the road. It was dark but I could see this dog, and I was thinking that John Dark did not see the dog. My hands and arms would not move, and my mouth would not speak. I wanted to say something but nothing happened. I sadly sat there, as that poor dog was run over. If a teacher called on me to speak in class, this was the same type of coma that would come over me. In this state, I would not feel my pain, but I felt for that dog, and I could do nothing.

One day, Sally told me that she was going bowling after school, and I was going to walk there after school and meet her for the first time unsupervised. I was very emotionally damaged and I could not understand the difference in Sally with her friends, and just Sally and me sitting on the couch together. When we sat on the couch together, my anxiety would go away for a little while, and I felt normal, peaceful. My brain could not process this and I did not see Sally again for a year or two. I talked with John again, and this time he had a girl named Meredith, who was five years older than me. Meredith was 19 years old. John picked up Meredith and me and took us to a Global Van Lines warehouse. John Dark drove a moving van for Global Van Nuys, and he had a warehouse key. John took out a mattress that was stored there for a customer, and John used Meredith to explain to me the parts of a woman's body, and for the first time, I had sex with a woman. This happened one more time with Meredith at another location. Meredith got into a terrible automobile accident, and we did not get together again. John had another girl for me, and he took me to her home. There was a girl there about my age, but that was not the girl. This girl's mom wanted to share me with John, and she too was looking at me with a smile. This was a very uncomfortable situation, her daughter was also uncomfortable with what was unfolding.

John tried to trade me with another pedophile, a man named Don. Don was a stunt rider for the movies, and he also liked young boys. I did not meet with Don, but I did learn a bit about their pedophile network. When John would come to our home for me, I would try to hide, and my mom would ask my older sister to find me. I would tell my mom while John was standing there, I did not want to go. My mom, John's coffee drinking partner, would tell me to go. One time, after my breakdown, my mom went into therapy with me. My therapist, Alison, asked my mom why she would send me with John when I told her that I did not want to go? My mom said that my father wanted nothing to do with me, I was so depressed, she felt that I needed a father figure.

CHAPTER 5

Teenage Years

I do not know when John Dark started to molest my brother, I never did see them alone together. I was away from home as much as possible, so I just do not know. I knew that my brother, at eleven years old, was spending time at our neighbor's house. The woman was married to a fireman, and when he was gone, my brother was there. I found out later that she was molesting my brother. I did know that my brother and his friend would have sex with that friend's sister. I could just imagine the shit in that family. I think that 11 or 12 years old is when John Dark was molesting my brother. I believe that the physical abuse of my brother, and the sexual abuse, took a terrible toll on his life. My brother ran away from home at thirteen or fourteen years old, and he became a child prostitute. I know that my brother was passed around with the Hollywood movie crowd. I met many of those people, singers, movie producers, and an owner of a gay magazine called Zipper. I went to the home of the owner of Zipper magazine, a man named Billy. I also went to the office of Zipper magazine and saw my brother and Billy. Billy, I later found out, was Billy Bayer, who was pretty well connected to many prominent people. My brother lived with Billy for a while.

I went to Billy Bayer's home on one occasion. When I got there, I did not see my brother, but there were a lot of young boys there, younger than me, and I was 16. Billy and another man wanted to talk to me, and we went into another room. I ended up walking out, and no one tried to stop me, and I never went back there again. On one occasion, when I went to see my brother, I got sodomized by a movie producer in a big house in the Hollywood Hills. At sixteen years old, this was the last time I was sodomized. For a while, my brother and other boys were housed in a home in Panorama City, about two miles from where we lived. I sometimes would visit my brother there. I saw stacks and stacks of photos of young nude boys, there were thousands of them there. My brother later told me that this other man was pimping six boys, one of them being him. My brother said that he was mostly pimped out to people from Hollywood, the Catholic Church, and wealthy businessmen. Later, my brother lived for a little while with the owner of a nut processing company. I think that he was finished, or his age finished him with child prostitution at the age of eighteen. Life was terribly cruel to him, and I was of little help to save him.

Over the years, to soothe his pains, my brother turned to drugs and alcohol, but his mind was going. My brother's ability to hold a job was impaired, and because of his anger, it was a challenge for me to be around him. My brother tried to kill someone at our parents' home. He also tried to poison my mom, and everyone was afraid to report it. I was told that someone in Simi Valley was left for dead from a beating that my brother gave him. Someone from the Simi Valley police department called me, and let me know that my brother was the prime suspect in a murder in Simi Valley. Someone beat a man to death at a company called Rain Masters, in Simi Valley. They had no evidence that it was my brother, and he did pass a lie detector test. For a while, my brother lived on the streets in Simi Valley.

I recently took my wife to a location where my brother had lived under some bushes. When we went there, most of the bushes had been cut away. My brother was having a difficult life, and he lashed out at me again. My brother broke into our shop and caused $257,000 in damage. My brother was arrested and finally received some help that he so badly needed. He was diagnosed with paranoid schizophrenia and was treated with medication. A deal was made between my brother, the state and me. Instead of going to prison, my brother would go into a program where he would receive counseling, medication {which he must stay on}, and Social

Security disability. Until they found housing for my brother, he was homeless in Ventura. Because of Social Security, my brother told me that he was a rich homeless man. There is a strong possibility that his paranoid schizophrenia was brought on by his childhood physical and sexual abuse. Mad In America, December 4, 2015, "Research shows sexual abuse may cause Schizophrenia." Reuters Health News, November 2, 2010, "Sexual abuse in childhood tied to Schizophrenia." The Mental Elf, July 1, 2011, "Child sexual abuse may be important cause of Schizophrenia." Postgraduate Medical Journal, August 2011, "Childhood sexual abuse and the development of Schizophrenia." After the arrest of my brother, we had no contact whatsoever until Sam Morgan located him.

After the arrest of John Dark, for the next few years, my brother and I spent some time together. I would pick up my brother once a month, and we would go to Pine Mountain Club. We would eat at a small pizza place and go for walks. This reminded us of when we were children, walking in the mountains of New Hampshire. Part of the agreement that my brother made was that he would not consume alcohol. When my brother started to drink beer, the medication did not work as well. I became too uncomfortable around him, so I did not see him for many years before his death. The last few years that my brother lived were better because of the government, but his life ended at 54 years of age from a heart attack. My brother is survived by a daughter that I do not know, and a nice son named Frankie, who my brother greatly loved. My brother once told me, "In this life, I am fucked." I tried to talk him out of that thinking, but except for a very few good things, I was sadly, mostly wrong.

#

I saw the movie "Saving Private Ryan," in which there is one scene that really emotionally troubles me to this day. There is a battle in a town, and an American soldier and a German soldier are engaged in hand to hand combat inside a house. The German soldier gets the better of the American soldier, and when the American soldier is down and on his back, the German soldier tries to soothe the American soldier. When the American soldier is starting to become calm, the German soldier sticks him with a knife. That scene, that terrible, deceitful scene, is so close to what it felt like to me, as I was being raped. There is a big difference from the scene in that movie, and being repeatedly sexually molested. A child molester can help you experience death many times.

#

While I walked to my two jobs, I did isometrics, and when I could, I ran. In high school, I went to 7am P.E., and my first class, which was electronics. I did not want to miss electronics, that teacher was very, very nice to me. In the next class, I would get my summons to report to the office, then I would leave school and go to work. I checked myself in and out of 3 high schools, which my parents never knew. North Hollywood High, Van Nuys, and Monroe. Later, when I worked out on the heavy bag in Fort Ord, it seemed like 200 people or more would watch me. I was small but very fast with my hands and feet. I never started one fight, but sometimes a bully would be a bully. I did not hurt anyone, but I was able to make it very clear that this was not a good idea for them. Thus ended being that type of a victim. At the age of 19, I no longer worked out much, long hours of work and marriage ended this.

The last job I had before entering the military was working at a gas station at the age of sixteen. This was a cut-rate gas station where we were regularly involved in price wars. The owner would make sure that we had the cheapest gas around. We also sold cigarettes and eggs by the dozen. Besides auto repairs, this was our business. We were full service, we checked the air in your tires, fluids, and we cleaned your windows, besides gassing up your car. We had many regular customers that I became friendly with. This one man, who was a piano teacher, was also a regular. He learned that I was interested in the possibility of learning the piano. I guess that he groomed me a little bit, as he was becoming friendly. He invited me to see his piano studio which was in his home. Strangely, after John Dark, I had not learned. I went to this man's home, and I was shown his piano studio which had two beautiful pianos. The man left me with the pianos for a while. He wanted to show me something, so I was called to another area of the home. The man had his pants off while he was masturbating and watching porno on a reel to reel old-style projector. He also had porno pictures laying around. I was asked if I wanted to join him. I asked if I could use the bathroom and I was told where it was. I promptly left him there, masturbating, as I left his house. I drove myself away, and I never saw that man again. He was a piano teacher, probably around many children. Why did I not go to the police? I should have gone to the police. There are many, many articles about this subject. If you are raped or sexually molested, there is a high chance that you will be victimized again. I had the boy on the bus that singled me out, the movie producer who sodomized me, the motorcycle stunt man, a few other men, and a few middle-aged women who made attempts. I think that I was marked, but I hear this is normal after you are victimized the first time.

#

How did the molestation from John Dark stop? I would like to think that I had something to do with this. But that may or may not be the truth. Some things were happening. I was getting older and staying away from home more, so if John Dark came by, I was not there. The terrible thought I have is that when I was not home, my brother was. It is positive that John Dark did molest my brother. As I was working out more and more, I was gaining confidence. Did this help? Maybe. I did not have sex with that last woman and John Dark, I was starting to say no. But what really happened, I am not sure. When I did see John Dark, he was with other boys. I was so shut down, that I never gave it a thought.

I bought my first car, a 57 Chevy at 15 years old. I paid $75, and it was a real piece of junk. I got it home, and I learned how to fix many things on a car at that time. I turned

16 years old on a Sunday, so I had to wait one more day to earn my driver's license. The car was almost ready, but I drove it too soon. The brakes were not repaired yet, and I soon found out how bad they were. I almost hit someone, but I made it home with no one getting hurt. I think John Dark was thinking that I might talk, so he came to talk to me. John Dark had a 55 Ford Thunderbird that had a swapped out big block engine, which made his car pretty fast. John Dark asked me to keep his car for a few months, and I was allowed to drive it. In those days, there was a lot of street racing going on, so I raced the hell out of it. I disrespected that car, and I am not sure why, but I was starting to drive fast. When John Dark placed his car in my possession, I was not being molested any more, so why did he do this? I did not think about it then, but I do now. Was it an excuse to be around my brother, or a gift to help secure my silence? I think the time that he brandished his Winchester 30/30, was also a different way of saying 'do not talk.'

I went to school for a little bit, I worked at a Taco Bell, I cleaned apartments, and I worked out. Working out was number one, working was number two, school was number three. I was starting to come out of my shell, but it was not all good. Boys wanted to be around me because I had a car, and I could fight. Because I was going places with these other boys, I was around girls and they were everywhere. I believe that I only vibrated to dysfunctional people like me. I believe that every girl and boy that I hung around with had been sexually molested, just like me. I did not have time to work out, work, go to school, and socialize, so something had to go. Like so many terrible decisions, school had to go. But I was only going to school a little bit by then, so something else had to go. I had to cut back on my sleep. Now my life was working out, working, and so-called 'having fun.' Lack of sleep was a big issue, and I am lucky that I did not hurt or kill someone during this period. I would sometimes drive without any sleep for over two days. One time, I was driving with another boy in the car with me, and I blacked out. I was driving down Chase Street in Panorama City, not too fast, and I was losing my sight. I managed to get to the curb, and I just blacked out. One time, late at night, I was driving on the Hollywood freeway. In those years, there were no protective walls along that freeway, I was extremely tired, and I just drove off that freeway. I went down an embankment, but I did not roll the car. I ruined two tires and two wheel rims. I was so tired and so close to where I was going, I just slowly drove, and thumped my way back home.

I also had no real memories of this period of my life, most of these are coming back as this story unfolds. I believe that if I remembered much of this era, it would have linked my memory to my molestation, and I could not have that.

Many of the people that I hung around with were my age, 16 years old, and they drank alcohol and used drugs. I did not want to partake in this behavior, mainly because I just wanted to work out, that was my drug. See, part of me made some good decisions, maybe not for all the right reasons, but good decisions. The people that I hung around with thought they could fight, it was all in their mind, and when you add alcohol into the mix, you had instant assholes. The first fight they picked while I was with them, was outside a Cuban night club. They pushed one guy around and pissed him off. I was the smallest of these people, and my so-called friends backed away, leaving me facing this angry person. It was clear he wanted to hurt me. I tagged him on his face, head, and torso with my hands and feet, and he could not block anything. I never actually made contact with his body, so he was in no way physically hurt. I backed off, looked into his eyes, and I extended my hand. He actually shook my hand, and we all became friends. Thus started this stupid tag game. They told people that I could hit them 25 times, and they would not hit me one time. I was challenged many times over the next one and a half years, and I was never hit. This did not mean anything, and I did not look for or desire trouble, and I should put this in perspective.

I bought my first new car at 16 years old, and my second new car at 16 years old, I have no idea what I was thinking. My first new car was an AMC Gremlin, my second new car was an AMC Javelin. Funny, after I bought my first home at 19 years of age, and I got married, I could no longer afford the payments for that car anymore. I went back to a 57 Chevy, which was also a piece of crap.

The two boys that I hung around with the most were from Cuba. Their family had lived in Florida, then they moved to California, and owned a gas station. These were troubled kids, both into weightlifting and martial arts, and they looked impressive. One night, while I was driving with one of these boys, we picked up a hitchhiker. We dropped that boy off, and my friend got out of the car with him. My friend was talking to that boy, and then all of a sudden he hit that boy, just under his eye. I was absolutely shocked, and I started yelling at my friend. I told my friend that if he hit him again, then I would hit him. As I was arguing with my friend, that boy ran off. I do not know why I still hung around with these boys. At this point, they had started three fights which I had to help us get out of.

One night, I was driving with two boys and a girl named Sheryl. We stopped at a park, and one of these boys and Sheryl went off together, and the other boy and I hung around. When they got back, Sheryl got into the back seat, and the other two boys talked a bit. These two boys told me they wanted us to rape this girl. What the fuck?! Sheryl was just sitting there, listening to this shit. I told them that neither I nor they were going to rape Sheryl. They told me that they were going to rape her, with or without me. I told them again that they were not going to rape her. I received their threats, but I did not fucking back down. The bottom line is that we did not fight, and they did not rape that girl. Sheryl later thought that she loved me, but I did not want a girlfriend. Sometime later, Sheryl called me, crying. I went to see her and she looked like a raccoon, someone had beat her.

Her boyfriend had beat her, so I located and talked to him. As he was threatening me with a wrench in his hand, I calmly told him that if he ever hit her again, I was coming after him. Lucky for me, he did not have a gun, but when I talked to this girl a few months later, she had not been hit by him again.

Those two boys that wanted to rape that girl and caused so much trouble told me that they raped girls and robbed people while living in Miami, Florida. I was so lucky that I never drank or took drugs. I might have turned into the same fucking asshole as these two were. I did not drink, but these friends did. I was with two of these friends one night, and I was driving, of course. We stopped at a market, and there was a woman there, maybe 35 or 40 years old. My friends asked me to ask her if she would buy me some beer. I was 16 years old at this time, and I asked her if she would buy me some beer. She asked me to sit in her car, which I did. She told me that she would buy me beer, but I had to go to her home to drink the beer. I told this lady that I had two friends with me, and she finally said that they could go also. We followed her to her home, and we all went inside. My friends started drinking, and one of these boys was trying to seduce her in her bedroom. She was not resisting, so I left them there. She had an older daughter, who showed up with her boyfriend while we were there. A little chaos took place, and I made my friends leave. Later, my so-called friends were really interested in having sex with an older woman. They tried to talk me into going back to that woman's home, which I did not do.

There are some people who think that it might be good for a young boy to have sex with an older woman. Can someone explain to me how this could be healthy? In this case, what did this teach her older daughter? What does this teach a young boy? In my brother's case, that woman was married, and he was 11 years old. What also really, really sucks about this woman molesting my brother is her husband. Besides him being a fireman, he was really nice. He performed first aid on a head wound that I had received. I had been hit in the head with a rock, and I was bleeding profusely. He stopped the bleeding, patched me up, and then I was taken to the hospital for stitches. These two boys that I was with, well they were used to raping and robbing people, so I doubt that it would have altered them.

I knew a man who had been big in sports and was for a short time with the Dallas Cowboys. This man would brag to me that as a young boy, he would have sex with older women, including his teachers. Later in life, he was a bouncer, he was an alcoholic, he was a womanizer, and he died early in life. Check out Errol Flynn the movie star. He said that he had sex the first time at 12 years old with an older woman, how did that work out for him? What if I would have had sex with the older woman that John Dark wanted me to? How would it have affected her own daughter? What did I learn from the first girl that I had sex with while John Dark was there? I can say that II had no idea how to treat a healthy girl.

Where would these older women come from? We have seen many in the media, they seem to be married and have children.

These women just do not seem to be sitting around waiting for young boys to grow up a bit, then seduce them. They all seem to be dysfunctional to me, not a great role model. I believe that they are sick, just like John Dark, and they wait for an opportunity to come up. This is not the proper way to educate our children and help to maintain a healthy society.

A police detective from Van Nuys came to our home and asked me to go with him for questioning. I was ultimately handcuffed and arrested. While I was downstairs being processed, a police officer came down the stairs with four other officers. One officer was very angry with me, and he threatened to beat me up. It was claimed that I got away from him, and I had no idea what he was talking about. I did not say anything to them, I just listened. My brother later told me that while I was sleeping he took my extra car key, and my police explorer badge, and my car. I found out later that my friend had also been a police explorer, so he had his own badge. My brother and that boy, that hit the kid that I was arrested for, would make believe that they were undercover cops, and hassle people. They were actually chased one night, and they got away. I was questioned, and the police did not believe my version of the story, so they were going to bring the victim in. I was sitting down in a room, surrounded by about four police officers. When the victim came in, we talked, and that boy verified my story. I was let go and I never heard any more of this again. They did pick up my friend, but I have no idea what happened. Even if you try to be a good person, you need to be so careful about the people that you come to know. I was a loner for so long, people wanted to hang around me, and I was stupid.

Sometimes a boy named Mitch would hang around with us. He was a weightlifter and very strong. He had been in juvenile hall for having sex with a dog. The girl, Sheryl, who I saved from being raped and physically abused by her boyfriend, had also been in juvenile hall. Sheryl told me that many teenagers in juvenile hall had sex with animals. I am so lucky, with all that I went through, my mind did not leave me. Around the year 2011, I was at a doughnut shop in the San Fernando Valley, and a man came up to me. He thought that he knew me. Even though he and I were aged, I knew him. He was the man, Mitch, that would sometimes hang around with us. He was homeless, living outside, behind that doughnut shop. I went back at a later date to try and find him, but there was a locked gate that had been recently installed, and I never found Mitch again.

CHAPTER 6

Military Service

Sally contacted me and wanted to see me. I had not seen her for maybe a year, so I thought it would be nice to see her again. One thing led to another, we were older, and she wanted to have sex with me. We tried, but I was sexually dysfunctional. Sally was the only person in my childhood that I told about what happened with John Dark. She just put my face in her hands and she kissed me. I felt deeply ashamed, but I was so shocked by the kindness that she showed me. I later went to a jewelry store and bought her a diamond ring. This is the kind of dysfunction that I was developing. Just because a girl did not shame me when I told her that I had been molested, I wanted to marry her. In my mind, I had to figure out a way to support us. I had been taking flying lessons at Whiteman Airport, I wanted to become a pilot. As soon as I turned 17 years old, I went to the Air Force recruitment office. They were busy, I was impatient, so I walked out and went to the Army recruitment office where they talked to me right away. I had not finished high school, so they wanted to test me. I went to Anaheim and took what was supposed to be a many hour test. I flew through the test very quickly and then left. My father said an Army Colonel called and told him that I had very high test scores. I went back to the recruitment office where I was told, because of my test scores, I could have any job that the Army had. I wanted to fly helicopters, but the only way they could guarantee this job was if I had four years of college. The recruiter told me not to worry, with my scores, I would be accepted for flight school. I needed to pick a job, so I picked helicopter mechanic. If I could not fly them, I would fix them. I turned 17 years old in June of 1971, but I delayed going into the Army until September 1971. I worked a little longer, then I took one month off from work, and I took a vacation. I had worked some type of job since I was 13 years old. At one time in America, 13 years was maybe a bit old to start working, so it did not seem like a big deal to me.

A bunch of us guys were bussed up to Fort Ord from Los Angeles. There were a lot of unhappy people with me who had been drafted, and they did not want to be there. I thought that the whole thing was kind of cool, and that I would love the Army. I just enlisted to learn to fly and make a living. I remember that we were in line to receive some shots, and I was chosen to apply alcohol on one arm, while someone else had the other arm. These guys would get their shots, after taking about two steps, they were acting like babies. After I received my shots, I understood only one shot was an issue. You take about two steps, and oh shit, like many others, I did one arm jumping jacks the next day.

We were waiting in line for our haircuts and an officer yelled out, "Does anyone know how to play chess?" I don't know why, but I raised my arm. I was brought into a small room, and I was to play the Colonel. There was the Colonel, myself, and maybe 4 or 5 officers smoking and standing around a table. These other officers were betting money on who would win. I lost the first game, but I won the next two games. The officers were shaking my hand and patting my back. They said that I was the first person to beat the Colonel, and they made some money off me. When I finished boot camp, I was to look them up, and they would buy me a beer. I went back and I got my haircut.

I was in the Army at 17 years of age, doing my boot camp at Fort Ord, California. There was a big room which had many phone booths in it. There were lines for each phone booth, and this large room was full. I was on the phone and there were, of course, many people waiting for me to finish. When I finished, and the next boy could take his turn using the phone, another boy pushed past him and tried to enter the phone booth. I stopped that boy, and I told him that this other boy had been waiting for me. This person was very unhappy with me, and he started to explain all the not so nice things that he was going to do to me. I calmly told that person, let's go out and talk about this. This time, I did plan on a fight, but I was pretty stupid. Because of the danger of growing up in our home as a child, I had become very aware of people around me, becoming hypersensitive. I knew exactly where that boy was, behind me, following me outside. I was not interested in people watching us fight, so as I stepped out, I looked to the right and then the left. I caught it just in time as his fist hit me on the side of my head. I somehow ended up on the hood of a car, and I had him in a hold. I was barely conscious, and he was yelling to let him go. I was trying to clear my head, and there were a lot of people around. I was not thinking good thoughts, I was going to hurt that boy, but not with everybody there. I talked to that boy while I was holding him, and I finally let him go. We were both lucky that it did not go any further. As I think of this now, there is a big lesson here. Is there another way? I believe because of this incident, I had to successfully defend myself two more times at Fort Ord. The physical training helped me get through my difficult childhood, and was good for my health, and it came in handy a few times later in life. But I really, really wish that I had a mentor.

I actually really liked boot camp and received a special benefit. On one of my trips back home, I drove my new 1971 Javelin, and I parked it at a parking garage in Monterey. When my Sergeant found out about my car, he made me a deal. If he could drive my car, he would take me out on the town some evenings which sounded good to me. He brought my car on base and got base stickers for it. One day, I went to my car, popped the trunk, and holy shit, it was full of marijuana. I found the Sergeant and told him that he needed to get this out of my car. He said that he would take care of it. I do not know if he transported anymore weed with my car, but he still had possession of it.

We took some tests in boot camp and after my test, I was brought into a room to be talked to. Apparently, they thought that I was intelligent. I was told that with a little bit of study, I would qualify for West Point, but I would have to guarantee more time in the Army. I would not agree to do that, so I blew that opportunity. They took the top five people with the highest PT scores, and we finished boot camp early. I was number one in our company the first time that we tested, and a Korean friend of mine was number two. My Korean friend was a second-degree black belt, and we would sometimes relax and spar together. The second time that we were tested, I came in second place, and my Korean friend came in number one. This was fine with me, I liked that guy. They took us five guys with the top PT scores, and we went to some special classroom training.

While I was in this classroom training, Sally ran away with my older sister and came up to Monterey. Sally was pregnant, even though she tried to say that it was our baby, it was impossible that it could be my baby. The Army actually handled the issue, and they returned home. Shortly after this happened, I was called into the office. I was told that they had too many helicopter mechanics and I had two options. I could accept a job that the Army gave me, or, because of the breach of contract, I could leave the Army and receive an honorable discharge. I asked if I would be accepted for flight school, which I had applied for. They did not know, and I could not remain in limbo waiting. I did not know who to talk to. My Sergeant was AWOL, the Army was intending to arrest him on drug charges.

My Captain was arrested because of something stupid. When we went into the Army, there was a box. You were given a chance to put into this box whatever illegal paraphernalia that you brought into the Army, no questions asked. I was told that our Captain was selling paraphernalia, and he got caught. And I certainly had no interest in talking to my father. I was thinking that this Army life was not that big of a deal, so I decided to opt out, and in a little while I would join the Airforce. While I was a holdover, I was told that I was accepted for flight school, another opportunity I blew. Needless to say, I did not collect on my beer.

I got a two-day pass when I became a holdover, so I decided to drive home. When I got home, Sally gave me back the diamond ring that I had given her. I drove to Mulholland Drive, and I threw that fucking diamond ring over a cliff. Shit, I still had to make payments on that ring for a while. I did not go to sleep for the two days that I was gone. I thought that I would be able to sleep a lot in the Army, while I waited for my discharge papers. I got back to the base really tired, but instead of sleep, I got 48-hour guard duty. It is not as bad as it seems, you get four hours on and four hours off. My problem was that I had not received living quarters yet. Another guy who was a holdover like me, showed me where to sleep. Three of us slept in an empty barracks. I got assigned some interesting jobs as a holdover. I got one mile of the road outside of Fort Ord to clean. I got to clean out the apartment of my missing Sergeant, and he forgot to take all of his weed with him. I moved furniture, I got to charge a hill, where I was machine gunned, and gassed two times. I got to go down trails at night and was ambushed. I knew when the ambush was coming, it was near mud holes still littered with brass that had not been picked up, I guess from the previous ambush. The people who were supposed to ambush my buddy and I were noisy and I could hear them. Their Sergeant did not like my after-action report, and we were sent away from there.

If I was not out in the field, I was receiving my meals at the mess at A42, my old company. One day, I was still hungry, so I got into the chow line of another company, and I ate two lunches. During this holdover time, I was housed with two other holdovers in an empty barracks. Each night, those two other boys would smoke weed and act crazy. The one night that I had my two meals, I got very sick, and I was taken to the hospital. I apparently got food poisoning, "karma," I guess. I had a 105-degree fever with a painful stomach. I did not want to be there. I had been given a two-day pass, and I was going to drive home. For two days I only had broth and some jello, no big deal, food did not interest me. I saw the doctor and I told him that I wanted to leave, but I could not leave with that fever. I wanted to leave the next day, but my fever had to come down. There were about 40 guys in my room, so people would come around day and night and pop a thermometer in your mouth, and later come back to retrieve it. After they would pop it into my mouth and walk away, I would remove it from my mouth, and place it back in when they came back to me. I saw the doctor the next morning and my fever was 102 degrees, but he still did not want to discharge me, so I pleaded, and I got released. I went outside and waited for a cab, gave up waiting for the cab, and walked to my barracks in the rain. I packed some clothes and took a cab into Monterey to pick up my car, which was back in the old parking garage from before. Soon enough, I received my discharge papers, and this was the end of my very short Army career.

When I was honorably discharged from the Army because of a breach of contract at the age of 17, I wanted a job fast, before I signed up with the Airforce. I called my old Taco Bell boss who owned two Taco Bell stores. He needed a person at his Inglewood store, so I went to work there. The first week, there were two of us white boys working there. After the first week, I was the only white boy working there. I do not remember seeing one white customer come into our store. I was a white male in a black neighborhood, and I loved it there.

We would sometimes make a McDonalds run, and it was my turn to make that run. I went to McDonalds, which was very busy, and I was the only white person, and I think the shortest man that I could see. No one disrespected me, no one. The person at the counter also treated me like any other customer.

One night, I was taking out the trash and there were some boys hanging on my car. I confronted them about hanging on my car. They were not impressed with me, they just stared at me. I think they got a kick out of me, they were waiting for my manager. The manager came out and she introduced us all. These boys belonged to a gang called the Crips. These boys came around our store a lot, and I became friends with them. One of the boys played chess, and we went over to my manager's home and played chess there. I had gone back to North Hollywood high school and tried to finish. One day, two of the boys came by my school, looking for me. They looked tough, and they scared many people. I saw them and wondered why they were there. They wanted to go to the Palm Springs tramway, and they wanted to know if I wanted to go. I was never treated so kindly in California as when I was working at that Taco Bell, and hanging around those new friends. After I got a job in a print shop in Van Nuys, I ended up losing contact with them. I really loved those new friends, but I was working 14 hour days, plus Saturdays, so we drifted apart.

As I am telling this story, I started thinking, where in the hell was the prejudice that we see so much on television? Is this stuff that we see so much on tv, meant to divide us? I was never treated badly by my new friends or anybody that I met there. My manager at Taco Bell was a great inspiration to us, and we worked hard for her. I certainly did not treat anyone badly. Where did race discrimination come in? One night, a man came to my window, he did not say one word, he just pulled a gun out of his coat pocket. I looked at the gun, and it looked like it was smaller than a .38. I said to him, "that is a cool gun, is it a .32?" He looked at me with great surprise, and he said yes, and did I have any bullets? I told him sorry, I did not have any bullets for a .32. He opened the cylinder of his six shooter, and he showed me that he only had two bullets left. I again told him that I was sorry, and he put his gun back into his pocket, and he walked away. That man was also nice to me. I have had two businesses for a total of 37 years, and I have not witnessed any racial discrimination. I am sure that it is there, but I have not been exposed to it.

CHAPTER 7

Choices Under Duress

After my breakdown, I started to see a therapist, Alison, at least three times a week. I believe it was Alison who asked me, was John Dark still alive? I believe I found out that John Dark was alive through Sally, but nobody knew where he lived. I hired a big Italian private investigator named Paul to track down John Dark. John Dark was alive and living in Alhambra, California. Many times, I drove to the home of John Dark. I later found out that John Dark inherited his home from his aunt, who had been murdered right there in that home. I was also told by the person who helped John Dark move into this home, that the bloodstains from the murder were still on the walls and ceiling. After I had my stare out with John Dark, I was wondering when I killed him, how long would I be living in prison? I did not know what difference that would have mattered, if my death would be soon anyway.

I went to the home of John Williamson who was my lawyer. John had just finished up a multi-million dollar business deal for me. I explained to John what had happened, and what I planned to do. He felt that, under the circumstances, I might not spend much time in prison, but he asked, "Is there another way?" Another way, what does that mean, I never thought of another way. I still harbored the thought of killing John Dark.

I again drove to the home of John Dark, parked my vehicle, and started to walk to his front door with a loaded 44 magnum handgun. This was the very same handgun that I was, at one time going to use to end my life. Only this time, I knew what bullets I would use, 240 grain wadcutters. In the heat of passion, I could of. In the calm cool silence and only a few feet away, I realized that I did not possess the ability for cold blooded murder. Somewhere before I reached his front door, I snapped out of it, with the voice of John Williamson ringing in my ears. Is there another way? I turned around and went back to my vehicle, and I started down the road of 'another way.'

Shit, how do I do this? I have never done this before. At this point, this was a 30-year-old crime. Most of these crimes that I knew of, were in or around North Hollywood, so I went to the North Hollywood Police Department. The officer that I talked to was great to me, but here were my issues: There was a new law on the books, 803G, which said there is no statute of limitations for child molestation in California, and it was retroactive. This sounded great to me, but I needed proof and I needed more victims. I could have filled out a police report there, but they needed to make an arrest within one year, or my case would be gone forever. They, nor I, for that matter, could guarantee that we would have enough evidence in time.

I knew names of boys who I knew, and some that I suspected of being molested in the boy scout troop which I had belonged to. I went to the Boy Scout headquarters in San Fernando Valley. I spoke with a gentleman and told him my story. I gave him the list of names of the boys that I had, and he went to look us up. The man came back and told me that I had spelled some of the names wrong. I told this gentleman that John Dark was still out there, and likely still molesting boys. I needed help to stop and put this child molester away. This person at the Boy Scouts of America told me that they could not help me. I was just dumbfounded. Whatever they tried to teach us boys who joined the boy scouts, surely did not stick with these idiots. This person would not even give me the correct spelling of the names of the boys who I had spelled wrong. Trustworthy, Loyal, Helpful, Friendly, Courteous, Kind, Obedient, Cheerful, Brave, Clean, Reverent. What about this Boy Scout Law that they, and all of us, learned? They were more concerned with covering their own asses, while leaving the innocent children like the ones that they were entrusted with, exposed to the likes of John Dark. Okay, those assholes were not going to help me, what now? I needed another way to find some of those boys, so I went back to an expensive private investigator.

This was way over the head of Paul, the investigator that I used to find John Dark (who I believe Paul found through Sam Morgan), but Paul had an idea. Paul showed me a photo of a private investigator who was on the front page of a P.I. magazine. Paul told me that he was the best, and he was a retired L.A.P.D. detective. Paul hooked me up with Sam Morgan. I met with Sam Morgan and told him my story about John Dark. Sam aware that my brother, myself, and many other boys, had been sexually molested as youths by a man named John Dark. I gave Sam the list of names, and he did find some of the boys, and he actually interviewed a few of them.

I was starting to understand more about the 803G law. It was retroactive, so if you could bring enough evidence, it did not matter how old your case was. But there was a problem. There was talk that it was not constitutional to make it retroactive. This was going to be determined in the Supreme Court. If we convicted John Dark with only us older men, and the Supreme Court ruled against us, then John Dark would be let out of prison. I needed younger victims within the statute of limitations. I decided to pay Sam to follow John Dark. Besides Sam sometimes following John Dark, another female P.I. was involved, and myself. Sam talked to me about installing a tracking device on John Dark's car. It was explained to me that it would be a more effective solution than trying to follow John Dark. I ended up paying to have a tracking device placed in John Dark's vehicle. This device did not last long, it was found while he was having some work performed on his vehicle. I was later told by the L.A.P.D. that John Dark thought the tracking device was a bomb.

Before we lost the signal of the tracking device, we were able to establish some addresses that John Dark frequented. I found out that one home he frequently visited was the family of another child molester that I knew. I would go to that address often, to see if I could find out anything. I would park my car away from that home and just go for walks in their neighborhood. One time, John Dark pulled up at a home while I was parked there, with two very young boys. I felt that these two boys were way too young for John Dark, at least that's what I told myself. I called Sam Morgan, and I told him about the two boys in his vehicle. Hindsight tells me, that after the arrest of John Dark, I should have followed up on this.

I decided that I would alert John Dark's neighborhood that they were in the presence of a child molester. I am not sure what I was thinking when I came up with this idea, I almost got beat up by 5 or 6 men. It seemed that the ladies of his neighborhood liked him, not a surprise, the mothers of his victims also liked him. For spreading these rumors, one lady was especially angry with me. This lady had her husband, who then got his friends to confront me. They were like a little angry mob. I stood my ground while they confronted me. I talked to the men, and I know that they understood. That woman, who I think was his wife, was watching this happen. I could see the faces in these men start to soften, but he looked over to that lady, and he said that I had to leave. On one of the homes that I stopped at, a young boy, maybe about 11 or 12 years old, answered the door. I felt right away that this boy had issues. He stood at his door, while he and I talked together for a bit. We talked a lot about his neighbor, John Dark. We talked about his school, and I left believing that he might be one of John Dark's victims.

I went back to that neighborhood with Sam Morgan. We went to the home of that boy, and Sam just listened while the boy and I talked. Sam was feeling what I was feeling - we felt that it was possible that John Dark had gotten to him. During this second conversation with the boy, I was able to receive his phone number, so we could talk more on the phone. The boy wanted to talk, he was just scared. I think the boy was like me as a child, he needed a friend. While we were in his neighborhood, we went to a home where two ladies lived. I was told through one of my other trips to his neighborhood that these ladies knew John Dark well. We knocked on their door, and we started to talk to them. This was not a good idea, because one of the ladies exploded and went off on us, as she threatened to call the police. We went back to Sam's car, with this lady following and scolding us. We drove to the

Alhambra Police Department, and we let them know what had just happened. I believe the lady took down our license plate number, so if there was a police report, the Alhambra Police Department would have our story and phone numbers.

It seemed that after school this boy was alone at home. Sam set up a three-way phone conversation with the boy after his school hours. The boy was not aware that Sam was also listening in on our conversation. The boy was starting to become more comfortable with me, and I was feeling the pain in his voice. I did not force things too far, he was not ready, and he was very young. At this point, we were 100% convinced that this boy was a victim of John Dark. I felt that if we gave it time, the boy would open up to me. It is very rare, in my opinion, for boys that young to talk, but I have seen it happen.

When I was very young, John Dark was arrested for molesting a boy who was about 9 or 10 years old. This was the only boy I knew of that told someone. The D.A. who handled this case never interviewed any of the 5 or 6 boys who were brought to the trial, but left us to wait in the hall. We were brought to the trial because it was known that we had spent considerable time around John Dark. I think the trial was going badly and the D.A. came out very stressed. He was pacing back and forth, and then he came to us, and in a stressed-out way, he asked us if we had been sexually molested by John Dark. We looked at each other, and we all said no. That was our chance, we could have stopped John Dark right then and there. I did not think of that, I was just terrified that this would get out. I am absolutely sure that I was filled with shame, but I buried that memory also. After my breakdown, I wondered what happened to that brave boy. I believe the D.A. and the police force back then were not trained well enough. They missed a perfect opportunity, by not preparing their case properly, and to not work with us boys before the trial, is beyond me. I had told Kevin Becker about the prior arrest of John Dark, but Kevin could not find any record of it. I discussed this arrest with John Dark on our first sting operation, and he admitted his guilt. Kevin Becker then looked deeper in the archives and found the record of that arrest. This is a burden of shame which I carry with me forever.

Sam Morgan, without ever talking to me first, in my opinion, did a very stupid thing. With a detective from the Alhambra Police Department, they went to that boy's school. They pulled the boy out of class and interviewed him there in his school. That boy did what I did, and froze. He denied having anything to do with John Dark, and he denied what he told me on the phone, which had been recorded by Sam Morgan. I could not believe that Sam Morgan, to my mind, would do such a stupid thing. The boy wanted to talk, but not then, and certainly not in that setting. They shut the boy down, almost the same way that I was shut down. I was not comfortable with calling the boy again, as I felt it would only make matters worse. There are trained law enforcement officers, like Kevin Becker, who know how to make a boy feel comfortable, and it certainly was not that way. I had no idea why Sam Morgan would do something so stupid, but later on, I found out why.

Finding this boy almost caused me physical harm, I needed another way. Things were becoming a little stressed between Sam Morgan and me. I had paid him almost $30,000 at this point, and each time we'd find more evidence, it was never enough to involve the police. At this point, I was low on money, and according to Sam Morgan, I did not have enough evidence to talk to the police. We had 6 men at this time who would come forward, and some of these men and myself knew of other victims, but no young boys. I needed some divine inspiration, so a prayer yielded me an idea. People like John Dark are always in need of new victims. His current victims would either age out, or start to resist, which could be troublesome for John Dark. John Dark was not going to change, so there must be a trail of emotional carnage. Little did I imagine how expansive that trail of carnage had become.

CHAPTER 8

The Sting

To keep John Dark in prison, with or without 803G, I needed to find younger victims. I talked this over with Sally. John Dark was friends with many members of her family. Sally had two sons who I was hoping to talk to. Sally had a younger brother who was also a victim of John Dark. Her younger brother was, at this time, housed in a prison in the state of Nevada. I am not sure if I talked with one or both of Sally's sons. I am not sure if anything happened to one of her sons; the other son, I was pretty sure he had also been a victim of John Dark.

I was trying to figure out how to talk with the boy who was in prison in Nevada. I decided to go to the office of California State Senator Cathy Wright. I spoke with an aide to the Senator, who then spoke to Cathy Wright. Senator Cathy Wright said that they would do whatever they could to help me. I gave them the name of Sally's brother, and what prison he was at in Nevada. I was incredibly surprised and very pleased that the warden of that prison actually called me. We talked about what I was trying to do, and he was extremely interested. We talked about a paper on pedophila which I had read. This article claimed that 95% of the men in prison for violent crimes were sexually molested as children. The warden said that in his experience, he thought the number was closer to 100%. The warden then arranged for me to talk with this man. The man knew of other victims and one of them was his cousin. We exchanged a couple of letters, but then I lost contact with him.

I was able to obtain the phone number of his cousin's mom. I actually had known his mom when I was a teenager. I phoned the home of his parents, and I talked to them a bit. I asked if their son, Ron, was home. She told me that he had not been there for a very long time, but he was there now. I introduced myself to Ron, and he somehow instinctively knew why I called. He blurted out that if this is about John Dark, I am not talking about John Dark, and he hung up the phone. A few days later, his mom called me. After Ron hung up on me, he got drunk and he got into trouble. Ron was in the Sacramento jail and he wanted to talk to me. I would not be able to see Ron until the next week since he was allowed no more visits for this week.

I again went to the office of Senator Cathy Wright. The office of Cathy Wright somehow made arrangements for me to see Ron the next day. That evening, I drove up to Sacramento, and in case I needed it, I had in my possession a letter from Cathy Wright. The letter contained the name of a person with a phone number on it. The next morning, I was at the jail, waiting in a long line. As we were waiting in this long line, we were forced to evacuate the building. Another visitor thought she would be able to smuggle drugs inside their jail. The funny thing is, when we were outside, a woman came up to me and asked what was going on. I told her that someone was trying to bring in drugs, and we had to leave. That woman said something like Jesus, thank you, and then she left. When we were let back in and it was my turn to speak to an officer, I was denied access to Ron. He was allowed no more visitors that week, and my driver's license had expired. It seemed I was not taking care of everything in my life that needed to be done. I gave that officer the letter which I had brought with me, and he called the person who was in the letter. I could hear the person on the other end of the line say, let him in. The officer that I was talking to told that person that my license had also expired, but again I heard, let him in.

To my knowledge, I had never seen Ron before. He was much younger than me, but not young enough to ensure that John Dark would remain in prison if 803G was overturned. Ron said that if I could get him out, he would take me to more victims, including two boys who were very young. I borrowed the money and arranged for his bail. I was not sure what time Ron would be released; I was told maybe 12 midnight. I did not want to miss Ron being released from jail, so I waited outside the jail, just walking up and down the street in front of that jail. I did fall asleep once on the sidewalk, before Ron was released at about 5 A.M. I learned a lot from Ron on our trip back to Simi Valley. I knew that John Dark was a prolific child molester, but I did not know that he also knew how to find male child prostitutes. I now wonder how my brother became a child prostitute? Both my brother and John Dark have since died; perhaps I will never learn the answer to this question. Ron had spent a summer driving with John Dark across the country, delivering boats. John Dark knew how to pick up young boys in many cities. Ron told me of many boys over the years that John Dark molested, but he did not remember all of their names or where they lived. Ron knew exactly where one of the families lived that had a boy who was plenty young enough.

We went to the home of David, and I was introduced to his mother and father. David was not living there anymore, and we did not talk about John Dark. These people had been a long-time friend of John Dark, so I did not want to have a confrontation with them. They told me on our next visit that they knew it was about John Dark. Funny how this works, Ron knew without me telling them, and Ed and Lori knew, without me telling them. It was quite obvious that Ron, Ed, and Lori were long-time friends. Ed and Lori were for many, many years, close friends with John Dark. Ed and Lori did the same thing that my parents did. They opened their home for John Dark.

They were rewarded for their friendship towards John Dark by the almost total destruction of their son. Their friendship ended when Ed suspected that John Dark was molesting David. Ed threatened John Dark, should he ever come around them or their son, again. David never admitted to being molested by John Dark to his father, Ed, which is consistent with us boys. Ed just felt that David was being molested.

Ed told me one time that he and John Dark were together watching TV. There was a report of either a rape or a child molestation. Ed said to John Dark, "how could someone do that type of thing?" John Dark said to Ed, "well bubba, there are a lot of bad people in this world." Ed told me of another boy that was David's friend, who also spent time with John Dark. Ed took me to the home of this boy, and I met the boy's father. His son was 18 or 19 years old and did not live there anymore. Ed had advised me that this man does not let anyone in his home. As we were talking to this man, outside, he let us in his house. I learned that this man needed to get away from his abusive father, so at the age of 16, he ran away from home. This man forged papers concerning his age and he joined the Marines. I should add that this man was not very tall, but he had very, very broad shoulders. This man was a Marine sniper in Vietnam, and I could see and feel that he was still traumatized by all of his life experiences. It seemed like he had built a fort of his house, and I could see things around that could be used as weapons. As the man was talking to me, he said that he could feel I was no stranger to trauma, and he seemed comfortable talking with me. I cannot help but feel so sad for this man. I believe he tried his best to protect his son from the evil in this world. No matter how much of a defense you have, something will come slithering in. John Dark might have been what slithered in. I should add that John Dark was a very adept piece of evil. As I type this, I now feel like I was some kind of a Grim Reaper when I went to his home. I now wonder what the balance sheet looks like for all that I did.

I was told by one victim who lived with John Dark for a while, John Dark would come home with different boys and molest them while he was there. I am not sure if these boys were child prostitutes or other boys that he knew. After my brother ran away, John Dark drove by our home, and he saw me outside. John asked if he could talk to me. I sat in his car as he asked me if I knew where my brother was. I did not know where my brother was, he just did not come home one day. I did not look hard for my brother, I only asked some people who knew him if they had any idea where he was. I feel a little guilty because I could sleep better when he was gone. I later found out that this was when my brother started his life as a child prostitute, at maybe 13 or 14 years old. I am also thinking that John Dark had been secretly seeing my brother. As I was sitting in John Dark's car, my father came up to us. I had my side door open, so my dad came to my side. My dad asked John Dark if he was having sex with my brother and John Dark said, "yes sir." My dad walked away, and he left me in that car with John Dark. My father never spoke to me about this.

I asked John Dark during the first sting operation if he remembered that day. John Dark said that he did, and he also said, while being recorded, that my father had said to him, "I tried that, but I did not like it." That is not actually how I remember that encounter. It is fathers like mine that helped John Dark to keep going. He did not want to get involved with his children's lives, he just did not want to be bothered. He did not even file a missing child police report for my brother. Maybe this, and the treatment that he gave his children, did eat him up inside because, for a second time, he tried to kill himself. This time when he was released from a mental hospital, he spent many years heavily medicated. My father would spend many years on a couch, completely covered in a blanket. You would not see him, we would communicate with him while he was hidden under his blanket.

I finally met David, and I asked if we could go for a walk and talk. David and I spoke a lot in metaphors. David was telling me about John Dark, without exactly saying that he was molested. We both talked about how we changed and the deep depression that we felt. But he just could not come out and say it. I was thinking that if David would talk to a therapist, he might be able to talk about this. David agreed to see my therapist, Alison. David took his girlfriend with him, and together they met with my therapist. My therapist was 100% convinced that David had never been molested by John Dark, and I was 100% convinced that he was. The truth is that David would not testify that he was molested by John Dark. However, the reason that John Dark remained in prison after the 803G was overturned by the Supreme Court, was because he, John Dark, admitted that he had molested David.

I had let Sam Morgan know that we were finding younger boys, and for some reason that I did not understand, Sam seemed to become more agitated with me. Sam wanted to talk at length with me, and he offered to fly us to Santa Barbara for lunch. I met Sam at the Van Nuys airport where he rented a Cessna airplane which he used to fly us to Santa Barbara for lunch. After we landed at the Santa Barbara airport, a Marine helicopter was also flown in. Sam and I went to talk with the two pilots. Sam had been a pilot in the military and he still had some type of a military card. This card was shown to the pilots, and they openly talked to us for a while. One of the men showed me around that Apache helicopter. During lunch, Sam told me that I still did not have enough evidence to involve the police. Sam also informed me that he felt that my life might be in danger. Sam felt that I might run into some terrible people who would want to stop me. He asked me to look into the Lincoln conspiracy. This was about a pedophile ring run out of Nebraska, involving many prominent people. Among other things, people had been murdered trying to expose this pedophile ring. Check out "*The Franklin Scandal,*" a book written by John DeCamp, and you will learn much about the message that Sam Morgan was trying to send me. Sam also told me that he could arrange for me to receive $100,000 if I would stop this case. I told Sam that John Dark will not stop molesting children, so I will not stop. I do not believe that we talked during our flight back, nor did I know why Sam was so angry with me. I did not look up the Lincoln pedophile case until many years later. I have no idea who or where that $100,000 would come from, I did not care, and I did not ask. Later on, I clearly understood why Sam wanted me to stop. I wonder if Sam had not been arrested, would my life really have been in danger?

I received a phone call from the Los Angeles District Attorney's office, concerning a letter that I had mailed them about this case. I was told that a detective Kevin Becker would be calling me. Kevin Becker was involved with a joint L.A.P.D. and F.B.I. task force to fight pedophilia. Kevin Becker called me, and during our first phone conversation, Kevin informed me that Sam Morgan was an L.A.P.D. detective. Kevin Becker knew about Sam Morgan, because it was in my letter that I mailed to the D.A.'s office. I informed Kevin that Sam Morgan was a retired L.A.P.D. detective. Kevin assured me that he was still active. I found that hard to believe because I had seen him on the front cover of a P.I. magazine. I simply did not want to believe this story of Sam Morgan being an active L.A.P.D. detective. With all that transpired, the thought of this was extremely stressful for me. Kevin could sense my stress so he told me he would look into it more, and that we would go over this when he came out to meet me.

Before Kevin Becker came out to meet me, and while I was driving, I received a phone call from someone from L.A.P.D. Internal Affairs. I do not remember the questions they asked me over the phone. The message was clear, they needed to talk to me. I drove myself straight over to the police station in North Hollywood. I met with two officers, and we went into a small office to talk. Our conversation was being recorded while they interviewed me. They showed me a mugshot, and they asked me if I recognized that person. I said yes, it was a photo of Sam Morgan. They were very interested in knowing why I was paying an L.A.P.D. detective for information. This was a bit of an uncomfortable situation, I did get a heads up from Kevin Becker, but I did not want to believe what he was telling me. I explained my story from the beginning. I told them how I met Sam Morgan and challenged them to check out that P.I. magazine. I had to go into various details, the places that we went, the people that we spoke to, etc. They did not ask and I did not tell them about the tracking device that was installed by Sam, but I was asked about that device sometime later. I sensed that when they were finished, I was not in trouble. Contrary to what Sam Morgan told me, Internal Affairs felt that I had plenty of evidence to file a police report against John Dark. To officially get the ball rolling, they took a report from me, against John Dark. The one year clock to file charges against John Dark was started.

My interview was only a little stressful, the outcome was that these officers from Internal Affairs treated me wonderfully. Everything I told them was the absolute truth, I just left that one thing out.

They also interviewed Ron. I think they wondered why someone in the banking industry was also involved with Sam Morgan. Ron had no involvement with the hiring of Sam Morgan. Sam found Ron, and together we went to the home of Ron to talk. I think being interviewed by Internal Affairs was way too much for Ron. I was later told that he had a nervous breakdown and that he was hospitalized. This person I also hurt, trying to put John Dark away. To my knowledge, Sam found two other victims, whose names I had given him, but I do not remember hearing about Internal Affairs contacting them. Although I probably told Internal Affairs about the other men.

I am wondering what went through Sam Morgan's mind. He took my money and acted like he cared. This was not a case of checking on a cheating husband, this was a professional child molester. I am sure that boys were being molested while he was doing this bullshit. Maybe he thought that he could make some money while developing a plan to make this all work out, I have no idea. I am sure that he got in way over his head, and he had not figured a reasonable way out, without being caught by his employer. He had to know that when a police report was made, he would be found out. Funny thing, Sam Morgan belonged to the Mormon Church, and John

Dark, at one time, belonged to the Mormon Church. How far would Sam Morgan have gone to save his career, and possible jail time? I am most pissed about that boy they pulled out of class. I was developing a trust with that boy. I believe that if I had a little more time with that boy, John Dark would have been cooked anyway. Children molested because of wasted time is on Sam Morgan's soul, not mine. Mr. Morgan can work this out with God.

When I had my first meeting with Kevin Becker, I was advised that they were getting ready to turn in Sam Morgan, but Internal Affairs got involved first, before this happened. Kevin Becker informed me that the evidence I had so far acquired might be tainted because of Sam Morgan. We needed to acquire more new evidence. Kevin Becker suggested that I try to contact John Dark. Kevin thought that if done right, John Dark would talk to me. If I could develop a dialog with John Dark, we might receive new evidence from the man himself. This information from Kevin Becker really knocked my dick in the dirt. In case I was successful in communicating with John Dark, Kevin Becker attached a recording device on one of our shop phones.

Kevin Becker had faith, but for me, this was a difficult time. I was separated from my wife. Because of my inability to manage, our company was doing poorly. My sleeping sucked; this had been very expensive; I aimlessly walked the streets at night; my nightmares were at a peak; our evidence was compromised; I got called into Internal Affairs of the L.A.P.D.

I had been kicked out of John Dark's neighborhood two times. I told everyone in his neighborhood that would listen, John Dark was a child molester. John Dark's neighbor had been pulled out of class, and asked about John Dark. John Dark saw me stand out in front of his home, staring at him. Many times, I staked out the home of another child molester who was a long-time friend of John Dark. This is where John Dark could have also seen me, when I saw him pull up with two young boys in his vehicle. We had installed a tracking device on his vehicle, which I later found out, John Dark thought was a bomb. To my knowledge, John Dark did not know that I walked up close to his door with a loaded handgun, which was a plus for me. Needless to say, my confidence level was not very high, thinking that John Dark would love to talk to me. I did the only reasonable thing that came to my mind. I went for a walk to the park and talked to God. I asked God if he would help me write a letter to John Dark, so that he and I could start a dialogue. I walked back to my shop, sat down, and dictated a letter from God to John Dark. I put this letter in an envelope, and drove myself with this letter to Alhambra. As luck would have it, John Dark's vehicle was parked on the street, with his window down just a crack. I inserted this letter into his vehicle. I drove straight back to my shop, and before I returned, John Dark had called me.

When John Dark called my shop, he left his phone number for me to call him back. I only had to turn on the recording device, dial his phone number and relax. Up to this point, Kevin Becker had talked to me many times, but it was a long road just getting here. John Dark was apprehensive about talking to me, but also very curious. I think he had a need for someone like me from his past, to talk to. I, and many other boys that were troubled when we were young, welcomed someone who would treat us nice. I still have problems today, realizing who is a good, or not so good a person. Maybe this is one of the reasons why so many victims will be revictimized in their life. We were so very vulnerable at one time, and it turns out John Dark was vulnerable this time. When John Dark victimized all of these boys, he could plainly see this was having a very negative effect on us. John Dark was like a psychopath, he could not feel, nor care about our pain. John Dark and I talked many times over the phone, but I could not get what Kevin Becker wanted and needed. Kevin Becker requested that John Dark and I meet somewhere to talk. Kevin Becker felt that if we met, John Dark would open up to me.

Kevin Becker proposed a location for John Dark and me to meet, and I proposed this place to John Dark. John Dark was not comfortable with that chosen location, so he proposed one for me. The location that John Dark proposed would not work for Kevin Becker. We went back and forth for a while, but we were at a deadlock. We had produced many stickers for a special model car. There had been a limited run on these model cars, and I had been given a finished packaged one as a gift from the manufacturer. I had told John what our business was and he liked cars, so I told him that I would give him one. I had gotten the address where John Dark worked at Disney, so I drove over there and gave it to a person who worked there. I knew at that time he was driving a truck for Disney, so I made sure that he was on the road when I got there. A very sad thing for me happened when I got there. John Dark had told the person that I handed the gift to about us being in contact after so many years. John Dark and I communicating after so many years, brought joy to him. This affected me very deeply, and I was starting to feel bad about myself. I knew that if I continued, John Dark's freedom would likely be over. I started to think of my brother and so many other victims, and the young boy neighbor of his, I just could not stop, but I still felt very sad.

We still could not agree on a location to meet, and then fate helped us out. Sally's grandmother died. This grandmother was at one time very close to John Dark, she treated him very much as her own son. I went many times to her home with John Dark, so I knew her well. I was told she wanted nothing more to do with John Dark because she found out that he was a child molester. That I know of, John Dark had molested at least three boys from her family, and used two girls to help keep boys. One of the boys ended up in prison in Nevada, and another boy was quite familiar with jails. This shit just kept happening, if a family did suspect or discovers the abuse, then it is difficult or emotionally impossible for the family to do anything. In the past If a family does want to do something, they are really confused as to what to do. It has not been that long ago, when we as a society started to understand, the tremendous damage done to our youth, from childhood sexual molestation.

This grandmother was buried at Valhalla Memorial Park Cemetery in North Hollywood, California. At this cemetery, she was buried near a water fountain. I checked it out, found her gravesite, and the water fountain was dry. I called Kevin Becker and told him of my idea. Kevin Becker checked it out, and he gave me the green light, and what timing would be good for him. I called John Dark and told him that this lady had just died, and where she was buried. I told John that I remembered that they had been friends for a very long time, and I suggested that this might be a good location for us to meet. John Dark agreed that this was a good location, so we worked out a date and time that fit Kevin Becker's needs. Because of the falling out that John Dark had with that lady, I was surprised that he agreed to meet me there. This could not have worked out more beautifully, her gravesite being so close to the water fountain, and the water fountain being dry, so the L.A.P.D. could record us talking without background noise from the water fountain. From a few feet away in her resting place, she could hear John Dark give the needed testimony to help put away a prolific child molester that spanned over four decades. She reached out from the grave to help put away an evil man who caused so much destruction to hers, and families of many, many, many other people.

I met Kevin Becker and to my surprise many other L.A.P.D. officers near the cemetery. My car was searched, and I was frisked because they did not want me to do something crazy like murder John Dark during their sting operation. I was set up with a wire, and I was instructed that they were concerned that John Dark might have caught on to me, and he might try to murder me. I was instructed that if I saw a gun on John Dark, I was to yell gun, and hit the ground. They told me that if they needed to, they would shoot him. I was stressed, I did not want them to kill him after all of this. Shit, I could have done that myself. They told me that they would just wing him, and I agreed just wing him. I think that John Dark being cuffed, and him facing past victims, would be worse than death. The L.A.P.D. invested considerable assets to obtain the needed evidence to put this career child molester away. They had a van to video and audio record the meeting. They had some officers posing as couples visiting gravesites, and they had a sniper. As I think of all they did to help us past and possible future victims, it makes me want to cry with gratitude. I love these people and I am sorry that I did not thank them enough. Without these officers, I think I would have gone into a deeper depression and just died. Without these officers, John Dark would have kept killing many more souls.

I sat alone for a while on the wall of that water fountain. There was a slight breeze, and I could hear a soda can move around inside of that dry water fountain. I stepped into the dry water fountain to retrieve the soda can, so the noise would not interfere with our conversation if John Dark arrived. John Dark's vehicle was finally driving up to the water fountain where I was sitting, waiting for him. As John Dark parked his vehicle, I stood up and walked over to him. I had the wire on, so I needed to be careful. John Dark wanted to hug me, I could not do that, he would be able to feel the device. I told John Dark that I was in a lot of pain, I had hurt my shoulder, so I extended my hand, and we just shook hands. We walked over to the water fountain wall, and we both sat down. As John Dark and I were sitting on the water fountain wall talking, there were people in the cemetery visiting gravesites. Many of these people were part of the L.A.P.D.

John Dark asked me what I wanted from him. I told him that I had repressed memories, and when my memory came back, I was very angry. I read some self-help books, and I told him the names of the books. I said that I came to believe that I needed to talk with him, to work through this, and he said he was willing to help me. We talked about a lot of small things unrelated to what I needed, but we were becoming comfortable talking to each other. I told him I guessed that starting at the age of twelve, he had sex with me about 100 times and he agreed. We talked about my brother, and he talked about how my brother was so angry. We talked about his relationship with a boy who was one year younger than me, and that boy's two brothers. I had learned that one of the brothers was six years old when John had sex with him, but John Dark would not admit to that boy being that young. These boys had lived with John Dark at one time in Canyon Country, and that boy would have been about six years old at that time. I talked to him about the boy that he had beat up because he was refusing him, but I did not bring up the time that he almost broke my arm. I did not bring up that he molested a young brother in front of an older brother. I did not bring up the boy that he molested at the silver knapsack camping trip, and that he later sodomized that boy right in front of me, or that this boy had a nervous breakdown after I talked to him. I did not talk to him about the boy that was still in prison. I did not talk about the boy that I bailed out of jail. I did not talk about the other boys from the Boy Scouts. I did not talk about the twins. I did not talk about David or his friend. I did not talk about other boys I was told about from when I talked to some of his other victims. We talked about other boys, but not specific sex acts, some of that would come later. I asked John Dark how he knew he could do to me what he did, at my age, and I would not say anything to anyone. John Dark said he just knew. I do not remember how long we talked, or exactly how many boys we talked about, but Kevin Becker was right, John Dark wanted to talk. John Dark was legally buried at that cemetery. After John Dark drove away, I walked back to Kevin Becker emotionally drained. Every officer looked at me, and I could see that they felt this almost as much as me.

A few days later, I told my father that John Dark had talked about this with me, and he showed no concern about his sons. He felt John Dark was stupid for talking to me. My father met me in our parking lot to tell me he did not molest someone who was close to me. I did not ask him if he did, but I did suspect. I told him that someone did, but he was not concerned, however, he should have been. My father was angry with me, and I did not see or talk to him or my mom for a long time. I think my father was thinking I would also try to put him in jail. Most of the parents of these victims were unable to deal with this when their children were young, or later in life, as the reality came out. As a society, we really need to focus on this disease. This is the proverbial elephant in the room.

I believe it could be argued that childhood sexual molestation is the number one cause of death in America. Death is not instant, but gradual, over fewer years than a normal lifespan. There is an article in ABC News, May 25, 2015, that suggests that a victim of childhood molestation has 10 to 20 years less life expectancy than normal. There is a study written in the US News and World Report, September 15, 2016, that claims that the life expectancy of a victim of childhood molestation is 47 years old. During these shortened years, life is usually not of good quality. Many of these victims end up as drug addicts, alcoholics, male or female prostitutes. Many go in and out of jails or prisons more than is normal. There are physical and mental health issues, more than normal. Their emotional level is usually at a young age, therefore it is difficult to maintain a healthy relationship. The ability to parent properly is usually diminished. Basically, they may just be a fucking mess.

Before I started vigorously exercising at the age of 13, I was very stressed out, and Kaiser Hospital diagnosed me with stomach ulcers. After I started to work out, I know of no physical health issues, except infections that came from John Dark, and injuries from sparring with other people. When this vigorous exercising stopped at the age of 19, because of long hours of work and marriage, symptoms started to happen. My stomach was burning again, and I started to have bloody noses. I would sometimes just keep bleeding and it was difficult to stop. My nose would keep running and I would have difficulty breathing at night. My eyes would crust over while I slept. I would wake up many times in the middle of the night, having to run hot water so I could breathe the vapor and breathe easier. I would use hot water to clean the crust out of my eyes, so I could see. I was starting to develop violent nightmares. During some of these nightmares, I would have terrible shakes. I absolutely could not be touched while I slept, this would cause way too much anxiety. I eventually started to have muscle spasms all over my body. Sometimes I would have a muscle twitch somewhere on my body that would last for days. Sometimes the muscle twitch would be on my face, and when it stopped, my face sagged in that area. I developed nerve issues in my head that would feel like a spike was driven into me. If I was walking when this happened, it might drop me to my knees. I kept pushing myself at work, sleep three or four hours and go back to work. I stood on the concrete floor for so many hours that my legs were in constant pain. I would wrap my legs in ace bandages each day which helped to reduce the pain. One day, I was so tired that I fell asleep with my ace bandages on. I woke up with elephant legs. I started to try out different types of shoes, and I found running shoes were the best. One particular brand worked the best, and I have stuck with that brand for over 30 years. I could actually run a machine at our shop for over 30 hours straight, get a little sleep and do it again. I could not stop pushing myself, just like in my youth when I could not stop punching the punching bag. I pushed myself close to death, before my mental breakdown.

Kevin Becker called me and requested another sting operation with John Dark. Kevin thought that our shop was a great location for this to happen. John Dark really liked the car that I gave him, and he was excited to come to our shop. We planned to have dinner at the shop while we talked. I made John Dark aware that we ran two shifts and there would be people working there. We would have the conference room available for us to eat and talk together. The conference room was facing the street, and had big windows. Many officers showed up, all in civilian clothes. Kevin had the van that recorded everything across the street with a clear line of sight. Many officers were posing as employees while John Dark was visiting there. Kevin Becker had worked with me, as to how he would like the conversation to flow. We needed to test that the sound and recording were working properly. An actual employee named George and I were to hold a conversation in the conference room. George knew what was happening and he volunteered to test the equipment with me. George thought he would discuss a crime he might have committed while being recorded. While we were waiting for John Dark to arrive, a customer showed up and made a joke. This customer saw extra cars, walked in and said, "What the hell is going on here, I have a trunk full of drugs." I tried to tell him that I was wired, and when he understood, he said "Jesus Christ," and took off. Jerry was a real good man, he neither sold nor used drugs. He was a Vietnam vet and I joked about this day to him for many years after.

When John Dark showed up, I gave him a tour of the shop and introduced him to everyone, including Kevin Becker, and the other police officers. John Dark and I excused ourselves to the conference room to talk. This time, Kevin Becker had me hone in on more details. Kevin wanted John Dark to talk about the different boys that I knew about, the sex acts, duration, places, etc. With one person, John Dark went into more detail about different things that he would do to that boy, and I became a little uncomfortable. I was afraid that I might become angry, so I excused myself to the bathroom. I needed to talk to Kevin Becker and receive more direction.

How can people like John Dark operate? He seems to have absolutely no feelings about what he does to all these children. No thought to the tremendous harm he does to their lives, or anyone around them. This is like pure evil that stings one victim, then another, then another, then another. I wonder, is there an age when they stop being a pedophile? We were trying to determine what age group John Dark was interested in and how young he would go. He did not admit to the six-year-old boy. The boy that I knew John Dark was arrested for, I believe was about ten years old. There was a competitor of ours, many years ago, who was caught by police having sex with two 13-year-old girls in his van. When they searched his home, among other things, there was a photo of his penis in a 6-month-old baby's mouth. I saw two young boys in John Dark's vehicle when I was tracking him, but I have no evidence if John Dark did anything to those boys. I was told that this other boy was 8 to 10 years old when he started molesting him, and that was one of the boys John Dark admitted to molesting. My brother was 11 or 12 years old. I am guessing that John Dark preferred 11 to 14-year-olds, however, if an opportunity presents itself, I am not sure how young is too young. I do not know how many boys John Dark molested in over 40 years. This other man and I counted about 78 that we knew or heard of. I am very confident that there were hundreds.

We ordered pizza, and when the pizza arrived, we took a break. John Dark spoke with a couple of people there, and I spoke with Kevin Becker. Kevin Becker was again right, as John Dark became more comfortable, he really wanted to talk. His stories kept flowing, and there was no sadness in him. I asked him, when these children got older, and he went to the next, did it bother him? I do not believe that it did at all. I had heard that Ted Bundy was part of a rape hotline at one time, can you imagine that? John Dark could do well on a child molestation hotline. Sitting there and listening to this very sick person, was just unbelievable, it was surreal.

Kevin Becker wanted me to do one more thing. Kevin wanted me to talk to John about David. I was trying to figure out how to work this in. The boys that I talked about had some links to me, that I could explain how I knew about them. David was unconnected, and I was a bit uncomfortable. I was trying to work this in, but I fell short. That boy was very important because, even if 803G was overturned, John Dark would not be released from prison. Kevin Becker later fixed that for me. When this was over, and John Dark left, one of the officers who was listening in said that he had wanted to come in and kill John Dark.

My job was done, it was all on Kevin Becker's shoulders now. That one year clock was almost up, and we had a lot of evidence. I was told that we had about 1,280 solid counts against John Dark. Each count carried 4, 6 or 8 years in prison, depending on what year they were committed. On the very last day, in the very last hour, Kevin Becker ran in the rain from one building to another in Los Angeles to file this case with just a few minutes to spare, before our clock ran out.

I am not sure what day John Dark was arrested on one of the properties of Disney, but I was told that he denied everything the L.A.P.D. had videotaped. I was told that when they searched his home, they found more evidence, but I was not privy to that new evidence. I do wonder what those people who ran me out of their neighborhood thought, as John Dark's home was being searched by the L.A.P.D., or when they never saw him again. I wonder how that boy, who lived in the home next to John Dark, is doing. I know that we saved boys from being molested by John Dark. I will never know who they are, or how many. There was never a doubt that John Dark would go to prison, Kevin Becker put together an airtight case.

Kevin Becker called and told me that bail was set at $1,950,000. I somehow learned that I could view his bail at the Twin Towers facility where John Dark was currently incarcerated. I drove to Twin Towers to view it myself. I went into a room that had another glassed-in room, inside of that room were sheriff's officers. I went past that room to where there was a counter with books that had names of the inmates and their set bails. I almost cried when I read John Dark, and the bail of $1,950,000. I so wanted that page, but I did not want to steal it. I went to the window where the officers were. One officer towered over me and in a deep voice he asked me what I wanted. I was trying not to cry as I was telling him my story. I helped put a career child molester in jail, and I told him what the bail was set for. I told him that it would mean a lot to me if I could have that page. At this time, other officers were listening in, and this man said in a soft, kind voice, sometimes a page will go missing, make that page go missing. I thanked them, walked over to that page, and that page went with me. After more than three years since I started on a path to stop this child molester, that page went with me.

CHAPTER 9

After Effects

We were ready for our first court date, which I believe was the preliminary hearing. The judge asked Susan Freeman how many counts they had. Susan shrugged her shoulders, looked at her papers and said a thousand - life. The judge cleared out everyone from the courtroom except John Dark, his attorney, Kevin Becker, Susan Freeman, the court reporter, an officer, the judge, and myself. I was to take the stand. I was sworn in as John Dark was trying to kill me with his eyes. John Dark and I mainly just stared at each other. John Dark could not say that he did not molest all of the boys, we had the recordings of him discussing some of his evil deeds, along with the matching testimonies from some of the victims. John Dark's lawyer instead, was somehow trying to make me the voluntary guilty party. I just calmly answered her questions, but not the way she wanted me to. The judge finally had enough of her shit, and he shut her down. John Dark broke his burning stare and hung his head. I was released from the stand, and everyone was let back into the courtroom. John Dark was to stand trial. John Dark was unable to raise the $1,950,000 to bail out, so he got to stay in his new Twin Tower home.

It took me many years to drive to John Dark's home again. I took my wife over there, after my son Weslee was gently pushing me to tell my story. John Dark's house is still there, there are bushes around the front of his yard that were not there before. The old street lamp that I was under, so John could clearly see me as we stared at each other, was still there. I showed my wife where I walked with my handgun, at John Dark's front door. I showed my wife where John Dark's vehicle was parked when I put the letter in from God to John Dark. As my wife and I walked the old neighborhood of John Dark, I showed her where the men came after me, and forced me to leave their neighborhood. I showed my wife where I was run out of the neighborhood the second time. I showed my wife where that young boy lived, who John Dark had befriended. I showed my wife the homes that I went to, knocking on their doors to alert them of a child molester in their neighborhood. The only person in that neighborhood who wanted to talk to me was that boy, and Sam Morgan had fucked that up.

My wife and I were married for more than five years, and she had not heard this story before. I simply was not talking about it, nor was I thinking about it. I had faded away from the victims and their families. I just crawled back into my box, and I took all of this back in with me. I only once celebrated the arrest and incarceration of John Dark. Ed, Lori, and I went to a restaurant called Rusty's in North Hollywood, which was a favorite eating place for John Dark. We felt that John Dark would never ever eat there again, and this was one of the best meals of my life. I did not talk about this to my family or friends. Except for law enforcement, the Los Angeles District Attorney's office, two therapists, the victims, and the families of a couple of the victims, there seemed to be little interest in John Dark, or what happened. Because not enough people are able to deal with this, I believe it is also one of the main reasons these evil crimes are such an epidemic in America.

As my memory was coming back, it was not a distant memory, it was almost real time, like I was living it now. It was more real now than before. I could shut it down so fast when I was a child, but it busted out, and there were pieces everywhere. There was no more comfort, I just had to take one step at a time. I did not think of living or dying, I just kept trudging on. I had more than my personal memories, I had the memories of many victims, which I could feel. I could feel me, and I could feel them. I had the memories of John Dark, the stories that he told me. I could envision the things that he told me, things that he did to those boys. I could feel the pain that was being inflicted all over the place by these motherfuckers. I know that these child molesters are everywhere. This is the biggest disease that I know of in America. This disease is a precursor of other diseases, like cancer, and mental illness. I bet that these fucking assholes welcome the illegal child immigrants into America, as fresh, vulnerable children for them to victimize. We need to yell at the tops of our lungs, "we are not supposed to fuck our children."

When I was the most sensitized to people who had been molested, I could not go anywhere without feeling stressed. When there was a Vons opened 24 hours a day, on Cochran Street, I would shop after 2AM. Twice I left my shopping cart in line with my groceries and left the store. The worst were the children, so many children affected me when I saw the sadness in their eyes, it was just like me, so long ago. I really believed it would be easy to find these child molesters. I thought I would be able to go into a classroom, know which children were being sexually abused, and law enforcement could take it from there. There are so many out there, where do you house these fucking assholes?

I found comfort feeding ducks. I would go to the 99 cent store and buy bags of bird feed, and almost every single day, I would feed the ducks. As soon as I was at the top of the hill looking down to the pond, the ducks and the geese would start squawking away. They could not get to me fast enough. They were all over me, some would sit on the bench with me. I could pet some of them at will; this was my little heaven. Two times when I was there, boys came by, and they were throwing stones at these ducks and geese. I confronted these boys both times, and I asked them to try and feed the ducks. I gave the boys bags of seed, and I was content to see these children transform from doing mean and evil acts to feeling joy as these ducks were responding to them. I brought a little joy into this world, and these boys and I parted under friendly terms. Sometimes, my son would go with me to feed the ducks and geese, which was a great pleasure for me.

I went to the court a second time. I do not remember who all was there. The judge blurted out, that this case is huge. I do not remember what was said at this time. Susan Freeman talked, John Dark's lawyer talked, the judge talked, then there was another date set. At some point, Susan Freeman talked to Scott, Ron, myself, and possibly others. Susan Freeman wanted to officially file only 54 counts. Susan Freeman said that if we filed the more than 1,280 counts which we had evidence for, there would be a media circus. This was fine with me, my only goal was to stop John Dark from hurting any more children. Anyway, 54 counts would put John Dark away for the rest of his life.

Shortly after being raped by John Dark, and the continual sexual molestation that followed, I had a dream, which became a recurring dream. I was on a very thin trail, on a mountain. This mountain was overlooking the ocean. About 1,000 feet below were jagged rocks, which were being lapped by ocean waves. I was more than afraid of falling, something inside of me was pushing me to go off this cliff. I was trying to hug and crawl into the mountain. I would always wake up with tremendous anxiety. As I am writing my story, I am wondering if this recurring dream was about me losing my mind. My brain was definitely scrambled, I could not think straight, and I could not figure things out like before.

After I was no longer punching the heavy bag or doing extensive exercising, I was having difficulty sleeping. One of the ways that I could sleep was to read war books and think of battles before I slept, which would calm me down. Before I slept, in my mind, I would prepare to go into battle. I would choose my weapons and ammo carefully. Most of the time I would fight alone. I would kill so many people who were trying to kill me, I mean sometimes thousands. The more that I killed, the more relaxed I got. When there was no one left for me to kill, I could sleep. In many ways this developed into a problem for me. I was starting to feel very bad about all the people I killed, so I had a new idea that seemed to work. I pretended that they were all actors, and after I killed them, and I went to sleep, they could get up. This worked fine, and I could repeat this movie day after day. I used the Alamo as one of my best battle grounds. I would bring my wagon, modern weapons, m16, a 45 caliber handgun, considerable ammo, and many hand grenades. There was one of me, but with modern weapons, I fought alone. I was either in a hide, or a foxhole, pretending to save the Alamo. I would later expand on that. This whole preparation and battle took a while each night, but I could sleep, except for the nightmares. The nightmares were always the same, someone was trying to kill me. One time, someone was chasing me with a handgun, and he blew the back of my head off. I literally heard a huge explosion in my head, I felt no pain though, and I woke up. This was the only time that I probably should have died in my dream. I would mainly have people come after me, and I would fight them in my dream. Many times I would have shakes, sometimes terrible shakes, and I would wake up drenched from sweating. My ex-wife said that sometimes sleeping with me was like being in an earthquake. One night when I lived alone, I shook so terribly that my ribs hurt for many days.

I have been trying to understand why thinking of being in battle calms me down. I do not like to see fights. I do not physically harm animals, or anybody. I do not like to kill insects. I did not spank my children, so why? I believe that when I was young, I was powerless. I would not fight off our father, I did not stop my rape, or the extended sexual abuse which was occuring to me. When I worked out on the heavy bag, I got some power back. I did not want to fight, but I got into fights. I was always calm, and to end a fight, I did not have to hurt anyone. Even when a man who I knew had killed a man before, came after me with a knife, I was calm. I was just fucked after I stopped my intense exercising. So I believe that I would fight whatever evil was coming after me, and then I was not powerless. I was still having nightmares up until December of 2018, which was a little more than three months into writing this book.

Another issue I had with sleep is that I could not be touched. But sometimes when my sons would fall asleep in bed with me, they could touch me, and I would sleep just fine. This was hurtful for my first wife, for more than 20 years of marriage, she could not touch me while I slept, nor could I touch her.

I always pushed myself, and I took too many risks in business. Sometimes we did financially well, and in the slow times, I did not make the right business decisions, and this would cause us to have financial hardships which were avoidable. I was always under pressure, but I just could not stop this. I had pushed the company to where we were the first in the industry for many things. Our process printed labels were second to none, and Dupont claimed that we were the benchmark in the industry. This constant pushing was destroying my family and killing me. The only times that I could feel comfort was with the thought of death. I thought I would get us back to a good financial position, so that my family was okay, and then kill myself. At one point, we had a cabin in the mountains, a place called Pine Mountain Club. Near our cabin you could take a dirt road into the mountains, then you would have to four-wheel a bit further to this real nice spot in the woods. This spot was like heaven to me, like our little heaven in the mountains, at our grandparents. I thought that this would be a wonderful location to die. I was going to drive there on a nice warm day, sit there for a bit, soak in the silence and then kill myself. I was going to use the same 44 Magnum handgun that I later walked up to John Dark's door with. I would think out the details carefully, except I never settled on which bullet to use. I had 240 grain wadcutters, and 180 grain hollow points. It really would not have mattered, but I just could not work out that one issue. I would be so relaxed and stress free, just by thinking about this. It was like death was my freedom, and I was going to heaven. I would daydream of doing this day after day, for a long, long time. Suddenly nothing mattered anymore. When the doctors gave me my death sentence, my freedom was coming, I was going home.

After my breakdown, I was not daydreaming or even thinking of suicide. However, one night, as I was trying to sleep, I was not consciously thinking of suicide, but there was a vote going on in my head. One part of me was trying to end my life, and there was another part, trying to say no, and I had NO say in this. My life was losing the battle, there were more and more neurons voting yes, and I had my 9 millimeter handgun loaded, a few inches away from me. I could not stop this voting, I was being taken over, and I was becoming very, very desperate. I had yellow pages in my condo and I was frantic. I grabbed the yellow pages, and I quickly found the suicide hotline. A lady with a soft, kind voice answered the phone, and the effect was immediate. In about 20 seconds, all thoughts of suicide had disappeared, and I felt very relaxed, like I had just been given a fast acting tranquilizer. I assured this lady that I was okay, and I thanked her many times. I have never had to call that number again.

The effect that lady had on me from the suicide hotline was the same that Sally had on me. I would calm down just like that, while I sat with Sally. Then, while I was emotionally drugged, John Dark could take me away to do his evil fucking deed. On one occasion, I was so stressed, but when I talked to Sally, I could feel the calmness actually move across my chest, until I was fully pain free. Of all of the times that John Dark took me to see Sally before he sexually molested me, Sally and I never even kissed.

CHAPTER 10

In a Daze

What now, what do I do now? Most of my time I spent thinking or doing something to stop John Dark. I was not sleeping any better and my nightmares were as bad as ever. More memories were coming back to me, with the sadness, pain and shame of my youth probably at a high point. I was going in and out of therapy. I aimlessly walked the streets at night. I would just keep walking and walking for many hours straight. Sometimes I would be a few miles from my home and be really tired. I would think 'shit, ok Raymond, one step at a time.' Many times, like me, I would see other men walking in the middle of the night. On one walk, I was walking towards a man who was very large, muscular, and had many tattoos. We were walking in different directions, but on the same side of the street. I was too tired to try and avoid him, and we were staring at each other. I could sense sadness in him, and as we got real close, we exchanged greetings. His voice was soft and kind, as was mine. At three A.M., I think he was also walking off some of his pain. I felt that it was possible that his childhood was similar to mine.

Of the many years that I walked alone at night in Simi Valley, I only had one incident, that I was aware of, that might have caused me problems. On this one night, I was walking back from the 24 hour gym to my shop, where I was now living. I would exercise and take my shower at this gym on Tapo Street in Simi Valley. Three men started to follow me, and I needed to go down Industrial Street which was very dark. I stood in the middle of Tapo Street, on my phone, talking to no one. I pointed to those three men, while acting like I was trying to explain to someone the situation I was in. Those assholes took off, and I walked back to my shop. After my breakdown, I had fallen low, I just could not seem to get back on track. My home for about two years at this point was the shop, and my companion was a cat. I wore out three cots, and was breaking in my fourth cot while sleeping there.

I was at a restaurant with a friend of mine, who owned a cosmetic filling company. I was telling my friend about me being molested as a child. My friend became very quiet, and he told me something that he said he had never told anyone before. He told me that as a child he belonged to the Catholic Church in Colombia. He explained that he had been molested by a priest. As he was telling me this story, he was crying right there in the restaurant. A friend of mine, who happens to be a black man, and I were talking about childhood molestation. He was a victim, and so was his sister. He thought he had worked through it, but as he was talking to me, he also started crying. I knew an Asian girl who was born and raised near San Francisco. She was molested from as far back as she could remember. She remembered that her mom, who knew that she was being sexually molested by family members, would perform vaginal inspections on her. She was so small that her mom would lay her on top of a washing machine to perform those vaginal inspections. From what I can tell, there is no race which is immune to childhood sexual molestation. As far as I am concerned, the only prerequisite is that they are young, vulnerable children.

I have a friend who is in boxing, and he asked me to meet his brother to talk about helping to promote a fight. I was sitting at a restaurant with his brother and his brother's girlfriend. Somehow I felt some trauma within his girlfriend, and I started to talk to her about her being sexually molested. Her boyfriend was shocked, and it looked like he wanted to beat me up. Her boyfriend had never heard about her experience with childhood sexual abuse. As far back as she could remember, she had been molested by her father, up until she left home at the age of 18. Her father, for more reasons than one, should have known that he was supposed to protect her instead of molest her. Her father was an L.A.P.D. officer. This lady was kind enough to find me a group therapy for victims of childhood molestation which I attended.

A lady named Lori worked for me, and one day her daughter came in to see her. I looked at her daughter, and somehow I knew that she was being sexually molested. When that girl left, I told Lori that her daughter was being molested. This was difficult for Lori to believe, but I called the Simi Valley Police Department. The Simi Valley Police Department had no tools available to investigate this crime without evidence. In a short period of time, this young girl had the courage to go to the police and tell her story. The Simi Valley Police Department did a good job using a phone sting operation to obtain evidence from that child molester. There was actually a police chase through Simi Valley, and they caught that man. This child molester was convicted and sent to prison.

I met a woman and was introduced to her 12-year-old daughter. I told the woman that her daughter was being sexually molested. I ultimately called Kevin Becker and he called the Los Angeles Sheriff's Department who went to her house. I do not know the outcome of that case, but a 44-year-old man was sexually molesting that girl.

I had a lawyer friend who was telling me about his two sons and his ex-wife. A man was helping his ex-wife and his sons, and a red flag went off in my head. I told my friend that I believed from what he told me, that at least one boy was being affected by that man. I told my lawyer friend that this man wanted his sons and not his ex-wife. I had never seen his sons or his ex-wife, I just knew. This man is now serving over 200 years in prison for child sexual molestation.

Tom worked for me, and while he was working, his girl-friend came to visit him, and I was introduced to her. When she left, I asked Tom who molested her. Tom was shocked, and he asked me how I knew. I said that I just did. Tom told me who had molested her.

Tucker was telling me about a 13-year-old girl that was being sexually molested. People knew, but they would do nothing to help this girl. I asked for information, and I said that I would take care of this, but nobody would give me any information.

I am no longer tapped into this deep understanding of victims. At this point, I cannot sense this anymore. The sad thing that I am pointing out is that people know, but for some reason, most of us seem to be so shocked and traumatized that we become unable to act, and I believe that these child molesters know this. I have met many parents of victims. From what I have seen, these parents experience terrible trauma themselves over their children being molested by a trusted person. I was so scared, asking my son, Weslee, if anything like this had happened to him. He assured me that neither he nor his brother Raymond had experienced this. I believe that if they had been molested, it would have been far worse on me than experiencing my own personal trauma.

I have seen parents emotionally crumble in front of me, trying to deal with this. The mother of the two boys who were involved with the man who is now serving over two hundred years in prison, committed suicide. I do not know what role, if any, that her sons' experiences with that man played with her decision to end her life. This is extremely difficult on both the caring parents and their children. What a perfect fucking crime, most victims will not talk, and most people who have reason to know, do not know what to do. And in the past you sure as hell could not count on youth organizations or churches to help you. I wonder, in our society which has a problem of this magnitude, who is running the show? Maybe I should tone some of this shit down. My experience with dealing with the Boy Scouts was long ago. I have little to no experience with the changes made in the Boy Scouts. I did not put my sons in the Boy Scouts, even though my wife at that time wanted to. We send our children to church, to worship together, to learn the bible together, to sing together, and we learn to forgive together. This is sometimes one hell of a test, to learn the power of forgiveness. Our priests, pastors, etc. will fuck our children, and I hear the same shit over and over on television. "Remember, we must forgive." What a cool fucking scam, when one of theirs gets caught, they just move that asshole around, and we can learn to forgive more and more.

I have spoken to many people who were victims and survivors of this crime, but I have yet to meet a person who experienced this sort of abuse and came out of it without some sort of serious emotional damage. In my experience, these people who were not abused, and try to say that this is not a serious issue, are absolutely full of shit.

I knew a girl, when I was 14 years old, a very beautiful girl, who was being sexually molested. It seemed that she was enjoying this relationship. She would brag about the size of his penis, and say that he only had one testical, but she loved her uncle. Many people knew about their relationship, and no one tried to stop it, including me. About 15 years ago, I saw her cousin and I asked him about her. He said that she was physically and mentally fucked up. I wonder if her uncle's wife ever found out that her husband was sexually molesting his niece. She was the only person that I knew during my youth who thought that they enjoyed what was happening. All of the other people that I knew were like me, they were bound by some invisible chain that was very difficult to break from. We all somehow felt deep shame, pain, and anger - maybe internal rage is a better description. We all seemed to come from families that were groomed just like us. Our parents, guardians, or people who should have known, seemed to all be disarmed by these highly skilled sadistic monsters. I do not know one person who asked for this as a child. The people who want to legalize pedophilia are in my mind, very, very, very, fucking sick assholes. This is another great way to help destroy our society. There are millions, and millions of victims in America who could have led a much happier, healthier life, and contributed much more to the health and wealth of this country. There are powerful evil forces out there, that want children available to them for their own deviant gratification. How could this have gone on for so long, in our youth organizations, churches, Hollywood, and our homes? I know from personal experience that Hollywood has many child molesters which has been an open secret for a long time. Some of these people make the products which our children are watching. How fucking scary is this shit?

CHAPTER 11

A Way Forward

We met at the office of Susan Freeman again. We were told that a plea deal was being worked out with John Dark. John Dark had cancer, and it was thought that John Dark would have just a few years left to live. It was agreed that John Dark would accept 15 years in prison, plead one count to each of us victims who came forward, and one count for David. David was very important, because if the Supreme Court ruled against making the 803G law retroactive, then John Dark would be set free. David would not have testified against John Dark, but John Dark did not know this fact. This meant that we would not have to endure a trial, and this would be finally over.

For the last time, we went to court with John Dark. The court performed their formalities and John Dark pled guilty. John Dark requested a certain prison to be housed at, and the judge said that was fine. It was over just like that, so many years of work, and more than four decades of him sexually molesting children. It was finally over. I had written a victim statement that I could read in court. I started to read my speech, but started crying, so Susan Freeman read my speech for me. As Susan Freeman read my speech (see below), I was bawling. Someone later told me that there was not a dry eye in that courtroom. After that, I was a little lost, I was spent.

Victim Statement

October 21, 2001

John,

I'm at the cemetery where we met a little over a year and a half ago at the very spot you and I sat at. I can actually see you driving up in your Ford Bronco, and feel some of the feelings which I felt during that meeting. I've come here quite a number of times over the last year and a half trying to work through some of my emotions and different things that we talked about. There's one thing that I just keep reflecting back to that probably troubles me the most. When you were here I asked how did you know that you could rape me and that I wouldn't tell anybody and that you could then move in and molest me for at least a year and a half. You explained it to me so calmly, so without feeling, like you were explaining a simple math problem. It's occurring to me that you were actually explaining how you could read a child and had developed the skills to rape and molest at will. You perfected your evil so well, I can't even imagine the damage you've caused in our society in over four decades of your child molestation career.

Did you ever take any time in the course of your life to reflect on these boys that you so badly hurt? Do you ever wonder what became of their lives? I'll share with you a little bit about my life. You were aware that I became very withdrawn, very shy and very scared. I soon could not look people in the eye or talk to people or even be around people. In class I couldn't speak out when the teacher called my name to respond to whatever the question was. P.E. class was especially humiliating to me because when they call out your name you're supposed to yell it out with conviction and basically I could just release a whisper. During every break and lunch time, I would just wander the halls and the school yard up and down, up and down, year after year. When I attended high school I usually attended one or two classes then would leave school for the remainder of the day. This caused me problems so I checked myself in and out of three high schools. Finally I just quit. When I turned seventeen I joined the army. Sometime around the age of thirteen I realized that if I kept moving I didn't feel a lot of pain. I started running and took up martial arts. I made up a work-out program that took up about 4 hours a day 7 days a week. I did this for close to 4 years. As a teenager I worked a lot. At one time I was employed by three different businesses. My whole life was consumed by working and working out.

When I got married I was a workaholic. I started my own business. For about fifteen years I maintained ninety hour work weeks. I didn't confide in people. I hid my emotions from everyone, I kind of buried that when I buried all the memory of you. I had two boys and my biggest regret in life is that I didn't spend enough time with them as they were growing up. When I wasn't working, so that I didn't have to sit and just think, I usually had ten or twelve books going at the same time. No matter where I sat in the house I could just pick up a book and start reading.

I developed some nerve disorders, breathing disorders, blood disorders. In 1995 and 1996, I saw three doctors. One of the doctors actually gave me a death sentence that I wouldn't be alive in 1998. All I could think of was, is it gonna take that long? In 1997 the memory of you came back and in a within a few days I had a nervous breakdown. Within a few months all of my symptoms were gone, you had been killing me from the inside out. I was on many different medications. I couldn't sleep, I had uncontrollable shakes. I had all I could do to get one or two hours of sleep a night. I lost 30 lbs the first few weeks, I reverted back to when I was a kid and just started walking four or five hours a night. Somewhere in this mess I still managed to come after you.

I have met many of your victims over the past few years, we have a lot in common. We had all been emotionally unhealthy. We all seem to sabotage any happiness we could have had. Some of your victims spent time in and out of jail, some had abused alcohol or drugs. We all have relationship problems, and we all did what you know so very well, we kept silent.

Your MO was almost always the same. You would locate a boy who was in pain which led you to a family in pain. You walked in like the hero. You befriended the family, gained their confidence, then move in for the kill. You sucked the life out of that poor child or children of that family and left them to carry out their living death. You could even infect multiple families at the same time or stay connected to a family for more than one generation. You infiltrated many organizations to get to boys. A baseball coach, Boy Scouts of America, Four Aces motorcycle club, the Mormon church, the Catholic church and the Woodcraft Rangers, a youth organization sponsored by Disney and other corporations. You took many boys to Disneyland using your free passes that you were given from your employment at Disney.

There's not a day that I don't think of you. Maybe they'll come a time when I'll go days where I don't think of you.

I harbor a lot of rage towards you. Rage for the damage that you did to so many young people, Rage for what you did to my brother, Rage for what you did to me. I have some anger towards some of those organizations. I reached out for their help and received none. I have anger towards a corrupt private investigator. If it were not for his criminal activities, you might have been stopped two years sooner.

I am grateful for much. I am very grateful that there were enough people that understand the dynamics of this type of crime and wrote laws like 803G, that have helped to stop people like you. I am very grateful to all the other victims I met that helped to stop you and the courage that they showed. I am very grateful for Ana Nuygen who works with senator Debra Ortiz, in Sacramento for all of her help and tremendous encouragement. I am very grateful for Kevin Becker of the LAPD, and the LAPD as a whole. Kevin understood my emotional state. He saw that you could still brainwash me even though I was in my forties. Kevin checked on me daily, even after your arrest. Without Kevin, I do not believe that you would be sitting here today. I'm very grateful for Susan Freemen at the D.A.'s office. Her kindness and concern are warmly appreciated.

We are all victims here. John, you had to live with your evil sickness. The boys you molested, the girls you involved in this, anybody that has a relationship with anybody who's been molested and hasn't dealt with it, their children, the parents of all these boys that you befriended and the cost you imposed on society because of the damage that you've done to so many young minds. I know not what else to do with people like you. You need to be stopped and you need to be away from society. You can't change on your own. You won't change on your own. A pedophile is simply a pedophile.

I'm very grateful, no matter what age I am, that this was able to happen and that I'm able to look you eye to eye and tell you what you did. I'm very grateful that you will never molest another young boy for the rest of your life.

William Osterhold, this I believe was the birth name of John Dark. When I was young, John Dark had told me that he had attended North Hollywood High School. I went to North Hollywood High School, and they allowed me to go through their school yearbooks. I found John Dark in a ROTC photo with the name of William Osterhold. On January 18, 2011 the Los Angeles Superior court filed a document. The people of the State of California V. John Dark { 7/1/1937} aka John Darkcloud aka William Osterhold. John Dark's parents were William L. and Maria L. Osterhold. I had been told in my youth that John Dark was in Camarillo State Hospital for a while. When he was let out of that hospital, he claimed that he changed his name to John Darkcloud. John Dark told me that he was related to an Indian Chief Gall, the same Chief Gall who helped kill General Custer at Little BigHorn. John Dark told me that he shortened his last name to Dark. I met John Dark's parents. His father was a big, stern, caucasian man, and his mom was a small, meek, Filipino woman. I later found out that members of John Dark's family knew that John Dark liked young boys, but to my knowledge not one person did anything to help any child.

John Dark had many different stories about his life. When I met him in the Boy Scouts, we were led to believe that he was a jet pilot, which was a lie. However he wore a real nice uniform with many medals. I heard him tell a story, that he had been a Green Beret, which was also a lie. He said that he had a private pilot's license, and if we were ever caught he would fly us out over the ocean, and we would run out of gas and then drown. John Dark said that he raced motorcycles. John Dark owned a 50cc dirt bike, and he belonged to the Four Aces motorcycle club. I went to some of the desert races with him, but I never saw him race. I also remember him molesting another boy at one of the Four Aces outings that I went to. I remember another pedophile from that club, and I know of another boy that he had molested from there. This other pedophile was also a motorcycle stunt rider for the movie industry.

John Dark was involved in the Mormon Church, the Catholic Church, the Boy Scouts, and the Woodcraft Rangers. I had been told that John Dark was involved in youth softball. The only job that I knew for sure was that John Dark was a truck driver. I remember him driving for a vitamin company, which was his job while I was in the Boy Scouts. John Dark later got a job at Global Van Lines. John Dark got me a job at 13 or 14 years old in the warehouse of Global Van Lines. I also was paid to make deliveries with John Dark. The other job that I was told that he held was at the tool shed for Disney, but at the time of his arrest, he was driving a truck for Disney.

Besides the many youth organizations which John Dark had joined, he used guns, motorcycles, chess, self defense, cars, and even that 18' Bayliner boat which was parked in front of his home, to lure, groom then ultimately rape and or sexual molest so many young children.

John Dark told me that he was in a prisoner of war camp in the Philippines during World War Two. According to John Dark's obituary, John Dark went into this camp at four years old with his father and was interned for 38 months. John Dark told me that he had been molested by a Catholic priest, but that he had enjoyed the closeness. I have no idea at what age John Dark had been molested or where he lived. I think being interned in that camp would have been hell. From what I could tell, William Osterhold was born September 11,1939 in Manila, Republic of the Philippines. John Dark died September 30, 2010 in Grants Pass Oregon.

Many years into his sentence, somehow John Dark was released early from prison, and he had not died of cancer. I was really not happy, so I tracked him down. First, he was released to Olive View Hospital in Sylmar, then to a more private facility close by. True to form, John Dark had convinced some staff at Olive View that he had been a war hero. I told Ed that I found John Dark, and he wanted to go with me to see him. I needed Ed to agree that if he went with me, he would not kill or hurt John Dark. Ed agreed, and he said that he just wanted to see John Dark and talk to him. We went to that facility, and they let us in to see him. When John Dark was arrested he was about 6'2" tall, maybe 225 pounds. John Dark was now bedridden, and he looked to be very much shorter, and maybe 120 pounds. I do not think that John Dark could talk, and it seemed clear to me that he would not be able to hurt children ever again. I stared at, but did not say one word to John Dark. I looked at Ed and said that I would be outside while he talked to John Dark. I felt like this was close to over, but I was having trouble trying to make a life for myself.

It would be many more dark years for me, before God sent me an Angel to save my life, and show me what it was like to feel loved. I told my wife that God sent part of my grandmother back within her, to me.

There is probably much that I will never learn about John Dark's life. I know from personal experience, and the testimony of other victims, that John Dark possessed an insatiable desire to fornicate with young children, mainly boys. I believe that his desired age was 11 to 14-year-old boys. I know that he sometimes sexually molested young girls, and many times used them to lure, or hold onto young boys. If it would help him keep a young boy under his control, he would use middle age women to perform sex acts with that boy. These willing older women were themselves child molesters, no better than John Dark. You have women in their mid-thirties, or forties that want to share young boys with another mid 30-year-old man, and I could see the excitement in their faces.

I believe that John Dark had a higher than average I.Q., but this intelligence was not used in a way to improve his life, or help society. Above all, in the art of manipulation, John Dark was a genius. John Dark had a way to make both male and female adults feel in awe of him. Can you imagine going to many adults in John Dark's neighborhood, advising them that he was a child molester, while there were children running around, and they would passionately protect him and attack me. To me, he could sodomize your son, as you were in a conversation with him, and these people would still not believe it. Not to the degree of John Dark, but this type of phenomenon happened with Larry Nassar, the sports doctor who was employed by Michigan State University [Chicago Tribune Sunday Nov. 25, 2018].

Where did John Dark find and groom all of these children? I believe that the vast majority of these children came from youth organizations, churches and from a family which he would have befriended. The Boy Scouts which John Dark belonged to, has quite a history of child molestation through the years. John Dark belonged to the Woodcraft Rangers, however, in my limited research of that organization, I have not found much history of child sexual abuse. If there is a very low incidence of this type of abuse in this organization, then they are doing something correct to stem this type of abuse. I did find an interesting article which involved children who were involved with the Woodcraft Rangers. Los Angeles Times December, 1987. An assistant professor of psychology at UCLA who teaches developmental adolescence, had to answer to 11 felony counts of sexual battery and lewd conduct against him.

John Dark belonged to the Four Aces motorcycle club. In my limited research, I did not see any published stories of child sexual abuse in this organization. However, I knew of two child molesters who belonged to that club. One was a rider, who also performed some motorcycle stunt riding in the movie industry, the other man was John Dark. I knew some boys who had been molested by John Dark, who he found because of their connection with that club.

John Dark belonged to the Boy Scouts. Well, I have considerable first-hand knowledge of boys and myself being molested while belonging to that organization. You could obtain many, many articles of this type of abuse over the years, concerning the Boy Scouts of America. I can attest to the fact that John Dark was quietly removed from that scout troop, with no charges filed. I can also attest to the fact that the Boy Scouts of America had no desire to help stop and bring to justice John Dark.

John Dark belonged to the Catholic Church. To my recollection, I do not have any first-hand knowledge of any boys that John Dark found while going to that Church. However, you could fill volumes of books which will show pervasive child sexual molestation in the Catholic Church.

John Dark, at one time, was supposed to belong to the Mormon Church. I know of three boys that John Dark molested who did belong to the Mormon Church, but I do not know if this is where John Dark first met them. With my limited knowledge, this type of abuse is not as pervasive as in the Catholic Church. There is an interesting article by Lee Hale July 16, 2018. "What happens when Mormon leaders treat child sexual abuse as a sin, not a crime."

I have been told that John Dark was involved with youth softball. I have no first-hand knowledge of any of his involvement in this organization.

I know of six other families which John Dark had befriended, and I am not aware as to how they first met. Two of these families, John Dark used their young daughters for some of his boys. One of these families, John Dark was molesting their young son, and he was arrested for that, but he got off. One of the families, their son endured long-term molestation. One of the families he used one daughter and molested at least three boys. One of the families, the boy started off molested first, then he turned into a child molester himself, just like John Dark had.

I had no first-hand knowledge about John Dark picking up young male prostitutes, but I was told by two victims that he had. One of the victims said that he picked up young boys from, I believe, Hollywood. One of the victims said that he picked them up in other cities while driving across the country. There was no internet then, I guess there was some type of underground network. Most of the time John Dark was a local truck driver, so I do not believe he would be able to afford the child sex slaves, someone like my brother.

John Dark may have seemed nice and kind to the outside world, but when you were under his control, he wanted you to do whatever he wanted, no questions asked. I was not the only boy who got physically hurt by this asshole. I knew of another boy who got beat up. John Dark used no protection doing what he did to these boys, so I am sure that I was not the only boy who received infections from him.

I remember a woman telling me one time, that she saw John Dark with many young boys that he was trying to help. This woman said to me that they were all like me. We were shy, and we had sad eyes. I wonder if that woman ever pieced this shit together?

I do not know how far John Dark would go if he thought that a boy was going to talk. One time, John Dark brandished his Winchester 30 30 to send me a message. I was told that some people believe that John Dark had killed a boy, but I have no evidence of this.

The last time that I saw John Dark before my breakdown was in Canyon Country. I would sometimes pick up this boy, to get him out of John Dark's house. When John Dark saw that I was outside his house, he went back inside his home. That boy later claimed that I saved him.

How many of these very serious ill people are out there, how many adults in this world feel that they have the right to fornicate with a child? I should say that from what I've studied, because someone is a pedophile - someone sexually stimulated by a child—they are not all child molesters. Some people know that this is wrong, and they somehow know how to control themselves. It's a sad situation for these people, and I hope that there will be treatment for them one day. This said, they seem to be everywhere. There are some pedophile rings that are so large, so huge, so well organized, that it blows my mind. Check out the by John DeCamp.

When I started to track John Dark in 1997, I did not see or hear much about child sexual molestation on television. We see more on television today, but much more on the internet. I am not sure if there is more child sexual molesta-tion happening today than 50 or 60 years ago. There seem to be a lot more child molesters caught today than before. But maybe this is because of modern technology and more effective law enforcement efforts. I am also thinking that it is not as easy as before for child molesters to enter organizations like the Boy Scouts, or even the church, and cause tremendous damage as before. I believe that there might be more pedophile rings than before because these sick people need their fix. We had child sex rings before, my brother was in one. But I believe that child molesters had more freedom back when I was a child. I think the child molestation that happens in the family between relatives and friends, might still be happening unchecked today. I believe that the vast majority of child molestation which takes place today is done in the home by a family member, or a family friend. But these child molesters need a way to get to more children. I have a sampling of articles, relating mainly to America. I have a couple of sample articles that go back more than 100 years.

- Joe Flood: Sherman Alexie and the Sexual Assault Legacy of Federal Native American Boarding Schools

- Indian Country Today: What has Caused the Most Cultural Harm to the Psyche of the American Indians

- "In 1996 Widman filed lawsuits on behalf of Dale and nearly 30 other residents against the Roman Catholic Diocese of Burlington, Vermont, Catholic Charities, and the Sisters of Providence.

- FBI: 'Epidemic' Levels of Pedophilia, Child Sex Trafficking: By Barbara Boland, July 30, 2015

- "Pedophilia in the U.S. is 'unprecedented' and has reached an almost 'epidemic level' according to assistant Division Chief Joseph Campbell.

- How Chance Discovery Of A Philippine Child - Sex Ring Helped FBI Close Book On Backpage.Com. By Edouard Morton April 21, 2018
- 474 Arrested, 28 Sexually Exploited Children Rescued During Statewide Human Trafficking Operation: LASD By Tracy Bloom, February 1, 2017
- Human-Trafficking Crackdown: 510 Arrested, 56 Rescued in California: By Jovana Lara January 30, 2018
- More Gangs Are Running Sex Trafficking Rings, By Leischen Stelter editor of public safety January 27, 2016.
- Hundreds Arrested in Massive Child Sex Ring in California, Including Entertainers, Community Leaders, and Clergy: Alex Hall November 26, 2018.

#

"The only thing necessary for the triumph of evil is that good men do nothing."

There are slightly less than four million babies born in America each year. If we do nothing, what will happen to the 500,000 babies born in America this year who will likely be sexually molested in their youth?

I have seen videos of thousands of turtles hatching at basically the same time. They run a gauntlet to the supposed safety of the ocean. On this short journey, there are many predators waiting for them. Many times very few make it to the ocean, and even if they make it to the waters, only about 1 in 1,000 make it to adulthood. Replace these turtles with human babies, and the ocean is 18 years old. We will also have a gauntlet to run, with many different types of predators. Some of us will be unloved, physically abused, emotionally abused, or sexually abused. Some of our brains will be very scrambled, a few thousand of us who were sexually molested will commit suicide. Many of us will not be able to develop the skills to thrive in adulthood, or marriage, or raising our own children. At a young age, many of us will run away from home and be subject to terrible horrors. We will be more likely to turn to drugs, alcohol, and crime. Many of us will turn to prostitution for survival. Many of us will develop serious mental disorders. Many of us will become homeless and lonely. Many of us will develop, more than average, physical ailments and diseases. Many of us will end up in prisons, and endure the nightmare of rape, and physical abuse again. Most likely by then, we are the living dead.

So what do we do? Please tell me, what do we do?

I believe that we need to wake up from this destructive nightmare that we are living. They say that it takes a village to raise a child. I feel that most of these villages have been asleep. We cannot arrest our way out of this. We cannot just rely on law enforcement alone, they are working hard on this, and they are continually becoming better trained. We cannot just rely on laws, shit there are laws for almost everything, which does not stop the person who wants to break them. The person who sexually molests children is more focused on developing better skills to not get caught, then laws being a deterrent for them to stop.

We need to wake up the entire village to this incredibly serious disease. We need a very sensitized population to properly attack these serious crimes that are going on in prostitution rings, child abduction cases, institutions, internet, serial child molesters, and where I believe most of this occurs, in the homes. We humans can be incredibly smart, and when we put our collective minds together, we are a force to be reckoned with. If we have the motivation, we can accomplish anything we put our minds to.

There are so many young to middle aged people who are so savvy on the internet, that with law enforcement, laws and their help, we could scrub these assholes from that platform. And as these assholes develop better skills, we will have a larger, more intelligent army to continue to fight these evil people.

If we are awake, we will automatically nurture our children better, and we will come up with ways to continue to reduce the hunting grounds of the people who are desirous of kidnapping and harming our children.

When we put children in any institution, we need to somehow figure out a way to stop the abuse which happens there. Remember, many of these children who end up in some of these institutions were so damaged by being a victim of this crime in the first place.

These serial child molesters who try to infiltrate every nook and cranny of our society where children are present are very, very fucking skilled at fucking all of us. They are no match for when we wake up, we will fuck them just like we did to John Dark and many others. We might deter the vast majority of these assholes, and they will have to find a healthier way to relieve their terrible internal stress. Maybe we will develop a cure for this very sick disease.

I am also very concerned about the children and families who are not in this country legally. They will need a very safe way to protect themselves from these serious predators. They will need a safe way to be able to report this. This situation is very complicated, but we have to work this out. The downside of not working this out is way too huge to ignore.

I feel that the most complicated area to massively reduce this crime is in the home. We can do this. Even as our mouths do not speak, our bodies do. I was sensitive to this at one time, but there are many people out there who are. As we talk about this more, educate ourselves more, we will figure this out. As we figure this out, we will create new ideas to better help the victims and survivors of this terrible abuse.

We have enough knowledge in this country to know that this crime is devastating. If we do this, we will help many, many people live healthier and more productive lives. We will reduce crimes, and many other costs for our society. We will be adding millions more young into our society who will create many things to help generations to come. There are some organizations out there that address some aspects of this problem, but I feel that we collectively have a long way to go, to resolve this terrible issue. We absolutely must do this, this is so big that our healthy future depends on it.

There are many, many articles about studies performed on people who were sexually molested as a child. Here is just a sample of these articles:

- Schizoprenia.com: June 16, 2006 "Children exposed to ongoing or frequent stress can suffer significant brain damage"
- "The long term effects of child sexual abuse" CFCA Paper No. 11 January 2013
- "The impact on child sexual abuse on mental health"
- "The Deleterious Effects of Child Abuse" Dr. Schwartz's weblog, by Allen Schwartz, LCSW, PHD For those who mistakenly believe that the damaging effects of child abuse are outgrown by childhood, this information may come as a painful surprise.
- "Keep Kids Safe" The Effects of Child Abuse on the Developing Brain.
- U.S. National Library of Medicine, August 2007: "Childhood Sexual Abuse and the Development of Schizophrenia"
- Reuters, November 10, 2010: "Sexual Abuse in Childhood Tied to Schizophrenia"
- Breaking News, Feb. 3, 2016: ISEPP by Noel Hunter, M.A., M.S., Doctoral Student "The Cause of Schizophrenia Finally Discovered" Trauma and Psychosis:
- December 28, 2018, Mad in America, Science, Psychiatry, and Social Justice: Research shows sexual abuse may cause Schizophrenia"

- "Sexual and Emotional Abuse Scar the Brain in Specific Ways" By Maia Szalavitz, June 05, 2013

173

CHAPTER 12

Children Groomed
For Evil Acts

My Definition of Rape

After a lot of soul searching, this is how I articulate my feeling and definition of rape.

Any person, man, woman, child, restrained either psychologically or physically for a period of time and enduring unwilling sexual penetration or other sexual acts, for the sole purpose of the needs of another or other living beings. This is extremely traumatic for the victim, and may be especially so for a child, who does not possess the maturity to effectively process this trauma, and betrayal. All of these victims will be left at least partially emotionally disabled, therefore be left scarred for the rest of their lives.

The Dynamics of Grooming

A friend of mine, Richard, and I were talking about this book that I am writing. Richard had read much of what I had written at this point. Richard explained to me that he had taught his boys to be aware of strangers, and where people should not touch them. I explained to Richard that yes, there are strangers who sexually molest children, but these are a small percentage. I was explaining to Richard how these predators operate, and as I was explaining this to Richard, I realized that I was explaining their art of grooming not just the child, but the family, extended family, and maybe a small community. This is not an art of grooming one person to take their money without having to use force. This is not an art of trying to induce you into buying a car, or furniture, or whatever, to part your money from you. This is not the art of trying to steal a kiss from a girl, or for her to agree to a date. This is the extremely evil grooming talent which they have developed to deceive many, many people and organizations, with the intent to rape or sexually molest for as long as they desire, yours or some other person's child. In the process, and as your child is being destroyed by this evil pathetic person, you will not question or deeply suspect this sociopathic son of a bitch. If, for some reason, which happens in a small percentage of cases, a child talks, you are more likely to believe this piece of shit than your own child.

I gave thought as to how John Dark groomed me and the other boys that I knew who were sexually molested by this piece of human shit. I also spent a considerable amount of time researching and reading articles about this subject from the internet. I am sure that every case is a little different from each other, and that there are different levels of grooming that are necessary.

If a child sexual predator buys a child from a child prostitution organization, like the one that my brother was sucked into, then there is no need to groom anyone. That child has long been groomed, and broken, and controlled. Just order them as you would a pizza. This child can and will be sold over and over again, with no hassle for the child molester. This piece of shit can be as dumb as dirt, with no special skills or talent needed. These children, though, are living some of the most horrible experiences that you can imagine. These children will be surrounded by people who will not nurture or care for them in a kind, loving way. As their minds and bodies grow, they will just be a twisted mass. They are absolutely thrown to the wolves. There is an interesting article called "Know the Facts" "Commercial sexual exploitation of Children" Chicago Alliance against Sexual Exploitation "The commercial exploitation of children is a large and growing concern around the world. Every year thousands of children are coerced, kidnapped or tricked by traffickers or pimps into the sex trade. Even though commercially sexually exploited children are routinely arrested as prostitutes and charged with prostitution in the United States, every act of prostitution where a child is involved is actually an act of child abuse, rape, and sexual exploitation." This article goes on to talk about many areas of this serious crime, and its effects on children.

Here are few other articles that I found concerning sex trafficking of children:

1. FBI " Epidemic" Levels of Pedophilia, Child Sex Trafficking by Barbara Boland, July 30, 2015

2. Massive Online Pedophile Ring Busted by Cops. Five Americans among 184 people arrested, 230 abused children taken to safety. Crime and Courts on NBC news.com

3. 474 arrested, 28 Sexually Exploited Children rescued during statewide human trafficking operation: LASD posted February 1, 2017

4. Global sex trafficking ring busted in one of America's happiest, safest cities. KCAL 9 CBS Los Angeles March 30, 2017

5. Largest Sex Trafficking Ring in Western US Busted. Children Openly Sold "In Plain Sight" Activist Post July 29, 2017, November 25, 2018

6. FBI Busts Sex Trafficking Ring Selling 3-month-old, 5-year-old sister for $600.00: Ray Bogan Fox News October 19, 2017

7. More Gangs are Running Sex Trafficking Rings by Leischen Stelter, editor of In Public Safety, January 27, 2016

8. 13 Sex Trafficking Statistics that put the worldwide problem into perspective. July 30, 2018

9. Multi-state child exploitation operation bust leads to 82 arrests, 17 rescues, officials say By Paulina Dedaj, Fox News

10. 238 Arrested in Major Hollywood Pedophile Ring Bust. The Department of Justice has just conducted a series of raids across Los Angeles and arrested 238 people in connection with a Hollywood pedophile network. By Jay Greenberg

11. The Link Between Prostitution and Sex Trafficking, Bureau of Public Affairs Washington, DC November 24, 2004

12. The Dark Origins of Pedophile Rings in the U.S., Youtube

13. More than 2,300 pedophiles are arrested across the country after three month online hunt for sex offenders, By Jennifer Smith for DailyMail.com June 13, 2018

14. Over 120 missing children found safe during Human Trafficking Sting October 9, 2018, By Tribune Media Wire

15. How chance discovery of a pedophile child-sex ring helped FBI close the book on Backpage.com Edouard Morton, April 21, 2018

16. Human-trafficking Crackdown: 501 arrested, 56 rescued in California, By Jovana Lera, January 30, 2018

17. Human trafficking victims mostly underage children within the U.S., By Perry Chiaramonte, Andrew Keiper, Fox News

18. Undertow of Exploitation: How teens get trapped in human trafficking, By Perry Chiaramonte, Andrew Keiper Fox News, May 18, 2019

19. Human trafficking victims recount tales of being forced into modern-day slavery "It was a living hell" by Perry Chiaramonte, Andrew Keiper, Fox News

Some child molesters will hunt and kidnap children for the purpose of raping them, or more. They do not need to groom anyone, but they need more skill than the assholes who purchase children from a child prostitution organization. They also need to learn how to perform their pathetic evil deed, and get away with it.

There is a lot of excitement for them, as they are getting a high off from just their hunting for a child. They have honed their skills, and they know when all elements are in line, to abduct a child. Where to take this child, rape or do whatever to this child, and where to drop off the child. Some of these children will never be seen again, but I believe that most will be let go. They have honed their skills to such a degree that they are capable of doing this with minimum chance of being caught. Here are a few articles about child molesters who abducted and murdered their victims:

1. Charges filed against suspect in April Tinsley case: Child Molestation Murder, Billy Kobin and Faith E. Pinho, Indianapolis Star published July 18, 2018.

2. Dean Corll, Wikipedia: Dean Arnold Corll {December 24, 1939 - August 8, 1973} was an American serial killer who, along with two teenaged accomplices named David Owen Brooks and Elmer Wayne Henley, Jr. abducted, raped, tortured, and murdered at least 28 teenage boys and young men in a series of killings between 1970 and 1973 in Houston, Texas.

3. Jeffrey Dahmer From Wikipedia. Jeffrey Lionel Dahmer {May 21, 1960 - November 28, 1994} also known as the Milwaukee Cannibal or The Milwaukee Monster, was an American serial killer and sex offender who committed the rape, murder, and dismemberment of 17 men and boys from 1978 to 1991. Many of his later murders involved necrophilia, cannibalism, and the permanent preservation of body parts - typically all or part of the skeleton.

4. John Wayne Gacy: Wikipedia; John Wayne Gacy {March 17, 1942 - May 10, 1994} Was an American serial killer and rapist who sexually assaulted, tortured and murdered at least 33 teenage boys and young men between 1972 and 1978 in Cook County, Illinois, a part of metropolitan Chicago.

5. 10 Terrible Cases of Kidnapping and Abuse, Rushfan, August 28, 2008.

6. What Happened to Robert Berchtold, The Accused Child Molester From 'Abducted In Plain Sight' February 4, 2019.

7. National Center For Missing & Exploited Children. Child Molesters Who Abduct: Summary of the Case in Point Series.

8. The common characteristics of child kidnappers will make you question everything. Julia Mullaney June 12, 2018.

9. Child Abduction - Murders: Why? Prime motivation is sexual assault, 44-State study finds. Sunday, October 01, 2000.

Many children were sexually molested in boarding homes, like the boarding schools for the American Indians, or homes like the one that was run in Vermont. You really do not need to groom the child, they have nowhere to go, or no one to listen to them, they are just fucked. Maybe the child molesters might need to charm other adults, or maybe not. This is probably also true in other institutions that children are sent to. Here are a few articles, concerning this topic:

1. What has Caused the Most Cultural Harm to the Psyche of the American Indians? By Sonny Skyhawk Oct. 29, 2012.

2. For decades, Nuns Brutally Abused and killed kids in Vermont Orphanage: By Amanda Arnold Aug. 27, 2018.

3. Wikipedia: Florida School For Boys; The Florida School for Boys, also known as the Arthur G. Dozier School for Boys {AGDS} was a reform school operated by the state of Florida in the Panhandle town of Merianna from January 1, 1900 to June 30, 2011. A second campus was opened in the town of Okeechobee in 1955. For a time, it was the largest juvenile reform institution in the United States. Throughout its 111-year history, the school gained a reputation for abuse, rapes, torture, and even murder of students by staff. Despite periodic investigations, changes of leadership, and promises to improve, the allegations of cruelty and abuse continued.

4. Staffers Raped Teen Boys at Juvenile Detention Center, Lawsuit Claims. Olivia Messer, March 08, 2018.

5. The Dark Secret of Juvenile Detention Centers by Josh Voorhees Sept. 03, 2014.

I believe that the vast majority of child sexual molestation happens right in the home. Whether it is a foster home, or their biological family home, right in the home. This could be a parent, guardian, grandfather, uncle, aunt, older sibling someone's boyfriend or girlfriend etc., but right in their home, with someone who would have reason to be there anyway. Each circumstance could be different, but they will need some level of skill, to pull off and get away with this while other people in that home should have known, or do know that this is happening. I have heard of, or been told, many stories by victims of their sexual abuse as children in their own homes, but this does not seem to get much media attention. I feel this will be the most challenging area of child sexual abuse to address. This is one or two children at a time, or in my mom's case four children. The other areas have hundreds of victims. Another enormous problem is that we might have a few million child molesters to deal with. This is a fucking problem. That also means that we might have a few million people who might try and block efforts to address this problem for their own self-preservation. In their eyes, 'fuck the victims,' which they already have.

I believe the real skill is developed by these assholes who started out as strangers, and were able to groom many people in a community and have a home or homes opened up to them, and then have access to their children. No one gets kidnapped or murdered, and most people are friendly with the child molester, as these children are being destroyed. These assholes will come to us through Churches, Boy Scouts, sports coaches, etc. This type of a person is what I experienced, and seems to be what most of the articles that I read talk about. I have no idea what percentage of children are molested by these particular evil diseased people, but I am sure far less than the ones who are sexually molested in their homes. However these assholes will sexually molest many more children in their lifetime than the ones in the family homes. Sometimes even hundreds of different children.

John Dark came on the scene as an over-achieving human being (or at least we thought). He impressed the scoutmasters, the scouts and the parents of the scouts. After he delivered his first speech, the scouts and the scoutmasters flocked around him to ask questions and hear his answers. We were like little puppies trying to receive the smallest of attention from this hero of a man. At this time, he was a fighter pilot, later on we were told that he had been a Green Beret. Many questions about the fighter jet he did not answer, he claimed was classified. I believe that he was involved in the ROTC, which probably taught him many different skills, but not flying a military jet fighter. At first, John spent much more time around the scoutmasters and their families, and not much time with the children. He was at ease with men, women, or children. He acquired many friends there. I know that there were at least two boys molested in that troop before me. The MO was the same, he was very friendly with the parents, long before he moved in for the kill. One of the boys he would take motorcycle riding, I am not sure what lure he used on the second boy. For me, he played chess, and he obtained permission from my father to come to our home to play chess with me.

John spent most of his time with my mother. My mom loved coffee, and so did John. My father was almost out of the picture and disinterested. Our father was not likely to sit with our mom and drink coffee and talk with her. John Dark found that void and filled it nicely. I believe this developed into a very important part of my mom's day. After my mom and John Dark became close friends, John posed the question to her. "May I take Raymond to my home to play chess with him?" He could focus more closely on my development of that game. That seemed like a good idea to my mom, and me, so off I went, never to return the same.

Unlike some stories which I have heard of, I do not remember John Dark trying to touch me before he raped me. I have heard of stories where the child molester will supposedly accidentally touch a child, to record a reaction. They will then work up to more touching, until the actual sexual molestation takes place. I had many adults come in contact with me, by touching my shoulder, or patting my back long before John Dark came along. None of these people who touched me before John Dark did anything sexually with me. I believe that John Dark went out of his way to not touch me before he raped me. I believe that by acting this way, he did not raise any red flags with my parents, family, people around us and myself.

I believe that long before he raped me, John Dark already had established that he could get to me, and other children in our little community. John Dark just needed a sufficient amount of time to groom everyone around me. He needed to disarm this small community, and make it safe for him to perform his rapings and molestation without getting caught. Before I was raped, John Dark knew our family dynamics and knew any people who would be around me. The first time John Dark touched me was maybe fifteen minutes before he raped me. I never saw it coming, I was so skillfully set up, I was fucked.

After I was raped, I had nowhere I felt I could turn to for help. He chose again the right family dynamics. It was like a child when you spin around and around and become dizzy. You fall down and the world is spinning around and around. I was not spinning fast, much more slowly. I could not stop the confusion and focus on any one thought. I did not snap out of this until a bit later, when John Dark found me, to comfort me. He was very, very skillful in the art of child sexual molestation, and child rape. With my family's approval, he just isolated me, and raped me. The isolation of the child is a very, very important part of their grooming.

Here are some articles which are worth reading:

1. Psychology Today: How Can We Spot a Child Molester? June 13, 2012 by Katherine Ramsland Ph.D.

2. Psychology Today: July 2003. The mind of a child molester you may have met convicted sex offender Alan X.

3. Psychology Today: Dale Hartley Ph.D. posted Feb. 13, 2019. How do serial child molesters hope to get away with it?

I really do not know what my mom thought of my changing, she took maybe a year to start questioning me. I was part of many conversations between my mom and John. It was believed that John should spend more time with me, to help me out of this state that I was in. My brother changed in a different way than me. He became more angry and outward, I became more quiet and withdrawn. It is so amazing to me that he could still come to our home, even after he was quietly let go from the boy scouts, and still continue his molesting ways.

This took a considerable amount of skill to suck everybody in and molest their children, and when that gig was up, he could move on to other organizations, and into more families, and get their children. John Dark is not alone, there are many, many, many more childmolesters out there just like him. He does not just destroy their children. He causes severe damage to the entire family structure.

When we moved to another home two doors down from the scoutmaster's home in North Hollywood, this was good for John, as there were three scoutmasters in a row. I think that the scout in the middle home was not molested by John, but the other boy and I were. John would visit both mothers for coffee, all the while carrying his coffee cup from home to home. He got free coffee and free children. I am not sure what MO he used on most of the other boys that he molested in that troop. I believe that he was friendly with all of the parents, but I do not know if it was just the moms. In John's neighborhood, the women were the most aggressive to me.

Even after John Dark was quietly removed from the Boy Scouts, no one seemed to talk about this, not one person. Many people remained friends with John Dark, and we as boys were never asked questions. What happened here, many, many people were sucked in. Why was there such a collective helplessness? Everybody got groomed! I am sure that many parents lived with extreme shame, and denial. And us children, we just tried to figure out how to live.

I really wonder now, how in the hell did someone like John Dark come to the Boy Scouts of America as a decorated military pilot, and not been vetted? What a fucking mess it was back then!

This is part of an article about the stages of grooming from "The National Center for Victims of Crime"

1. Identifying and targeting the victim
2. Gaining trust and access
3. Playing a role in the child's life
4. Isolating the child
5. Creating secrecy around the relationship
6. Initiating sexual contact
7. Controlling the relationship

These are some other interesting articles about child sexual grooming:

A. Grooming Children for Sexual Molestation By Gregory M. Weber
B. Wikipedia: Child Grooming
C. Were you "groomed," understanding the role of grooming behavior in sexual abuse October 5, 2017 by Heather Davidson
D. The Grooming Process - How Sexual Predators Con You And Your Child, Estey Bomberge
E. Educate Empower Kids.org, 8 ways a predator might groom your child
F. Child Refuge - The ways on how molesters groom their victims and how a parent can stop them

G. Child sexual abuse: 6 stages of grooming By. Dr. Michael Welner

H. Grooming: How child molesters create willing victims, By Laurie A. Grey copyright 2010

I. A profile of the child molester, By Rosemary Webb and Jennifer Mitchell

J. Understanding Sexual Grooming in Child Abuse Cases, Nov. 1, 2015, By Daniel Pollock

K. Two child sex offenders explain how they picked their targets/ wfaa.com 8 abc

Molester, 64, Gets 15 years in Prison for Decades- Old Crimes, Los Angeles Times Friday, October 26, 2001, by DALONDO MOULTRIE, Times Staff Writer

The End

Photo Section

My sister Debbie and I "happy."

My sister Debbie and I at the side of our grandparents home.

Grandparents home, my sister Debbie and I.

Our grandfather, grandmother, my sister Debbie and I.

Me ready for battle in our grandparents dining room.

Grandfather and Dad our homes are to the left out of the picture. This was our grandads company, and it did very well, until our father took over.

A front view of our grandparents home.

First home we moved into after being evicted out of our first
home. There were a lot of snakes there. { my friends}

A photo of me shortly before I was raped.

Troop three of North Hollywood, about the time of my rape.

This is me at 13 or 14, still being sexually molested.

I was in the Police Explorers in North Hollywood Ca.

A photo of me at 17 years old stationed at Fort Ord Ca.

That is the seat where John Dark and I sat through the first sting operation at Pierce brothers Valhalla memorial park & mortuary North Hollywood Ca.

My son Weslee, my mom, myself,
and my lovely wife Joanna

This book is not the end of the story...

in many ways this is just the beginning. We have a companion website for this book "feelthinktalk.com". We plan to develop a holistic approach to combat this terrible destructive disease, we call child sexual abuse. We plan to offer links to resources for victims, survivors, and people affected by this disease. May we grow as a community and effectively reduce these terrible crimes in our society.

CPSIA information can be obtained
at www.ICGtesting.com
Printed in the USA
FSHW010704020320